RESISTANCE IS *NOT* FUTILE!

The *Trek* Guide to Progressive Action

SCOTT ROBINSON

Copyright ©2024 by Paleos Media

ISBN 979-8345980392

Author photograph by Joshua Robinson

Remembering Vonda McIntyre,

by far the best of the Trek print writers

Also by Scott Robinson...

<u>Boldly Go!</u>
Star Trek and Humanism:
    Living by the *Star Trek* Ethos in a Troubled World
To Summon the Future:
    Celebrating *Trek* and Human Social Progress
Resistance is NOT Futile!
        A *Trek* Handbook for Progressive Action and
Resistance
Chasing the *Enterprise*:
    Achieving *Star Trek*'s Vision of the Human Future
12 *Trek* Rules for Living

<u>More *Trek*...</u>
    The AIs and Androids of *Star Trek*: The Technology of
    the 23rd Century
Be Like Spock! On Releasing Your Inner Vulcan
Star Trek Thought Experiments

<u>On Sci-Fi</u>
HAL 9000: An Unauthorized Biography
AI in Sci-Fi: Fictional Artificial Minds
    and the Real World Awaiting Them
To Everything That Might Have Been:
        A Philosophical Journey Through Space: 1999
Pluribus: Joy & Dread in the Benevolent Machine

<u>The Rock Candy Series</u>
Rock Candy: The Beatles
Rock Candy: The Beatles, Vol. II
Rock Candy: Elton John
Rock Candy: Def Leppard
Rock Candy: Millennials
Rock Candy: Boston

Table of Contents

*"It's been my experience that the prejudices people feel
about each other disappear when they
get to know each other."*

PRIME DIRECTIVES
Trek's Call to Commitment
99

"With the first link, the chain is forged. The first speech censored, the first thought forbidden, the first freedom denied, chains us all irrevocably."
Resisting Authoritarianism
101

"The first duty of every Starfleet officer is to the truth!"
Integrity in the Public Square
118

*"Leave any bigotry in your quarters.
There's no room for it on the bridge!"*
Racism and Social Inequality
125

*"When my status as a living being was in question,
you fought to protect my rights,
and for that I will always be grateful."*
Rights and Freedoms
146

*"The needs of the many outweigh
the needs of the few."*
Working for the Greater Good
161

Introduction:
Don't Be Assimilated!

We first became acquainted with the power of Federation democracy in "Journey to Babel" in the original series, when Kirk's *Enterprise* trucked more than 100 Federation delegates to a neutral planetoid to discuss and vote on the admission of Coridan to its ranks. We saw argument, contentiousness – and a serious, violent effort to disrupt the democratic process and usurp its outcome.

That's the nature of democracy. It's messy, it's uncomfortable – but it's better than the alternatives, as Winston Churchill famously assured us.

The idea of a self-governing society, where all are considered equal, is humankind's dream. It's one of the things that makes *Star Trek* so attractive to its tens of millions of fans. The Federation, which is wildly diverse and yet inspiringly united, is a utopia.

And especially now, as the opening decades of the 21st century have experienced an uncomfortable rise in authoritarianism – not just in the United States, but in Europe and South America as well. It doesn't look promising.

This book suggests that we can look to *Trek*, not only for inspiration, but for conviction and a call to action.

The problem we're facing will be outlined up front (in "The Library Computer: A Profile of Authoritarianism". Rising authoritarianism is cyclic, and even though we haven't experienced all that much of it at home, it has been part of the human story for millennia. We know what to look for.

From there, the book is divided into two sections. The first – "On the Away Team" –focuses on action we can all take to make our resistance real. Action that can push back against authoritarian abuses and overreach. Action that can reset the scales, tipping them back in favor of democracy. Action inspired by courageous and compassionate moments from *Trek*.

The second section, "Prime Directives", reviews the principles and values that are essential to embrace in resisting authoritarianism. These are *Trek* values, one and all, to be sure; and they are also humanist values, which should surprise no reader – *Trek* is, after all, a humanist manifesto above all else. Put another way, this is a summary of *why* we answer the call of the Away Team.

The *Trek* principles and values are based on some content published in two previous books, *Star Trek and Humanism* and *To Summon the Future*, both by the author. The calls to action have several important sources:

- *On Tyranny: Twenty Lessons from the Twentieth Century*, by Timothy Snyder
- *The Bill of Obligations: The Ten Habits of Good Citizens*, by Richard Haass
- *"The Authoritarian Regime Survival Guide"*, by Martin Mycielski[1]

Each of these is well worth the reader's time, for deeper exploration of these ideas.

It's my hope that this book will both inform and inspire every reader, *Trek* fan or otherwise, who is troubled by the direction the world is going and wants to do something about

---

[1] Found at https://verfassungsblog.de/the-authoritarian-regime-survival-guide

it. We've spent years, in some cases decades, admiring the courage and determination and resolve of our Starfleet heroes, with their firm principles and deep values. History is presenting us with the opportunity to follow in their steps!

STR
November 2024

From the Library Computer:
Approaching Tyranny

In 1930, Kirk and Spock search for clues as to how a deranged McCoy, having traveled back to Depression-era New York City through the Guardian of Forever, had ended the existence of the Federation.[2]

Spock refers to his stone-knives-and-bearskins-enhanced tricorder:

"This is how history went after McCoy changed it," Spock explains. "Here, in the late 1930s. A growing pacifist movement whose influence delayed the United States' entry into the Second World War. While peace negotiations dragged on, Germany had time to complete its heavy-water experiments."

"Germany. Fascism. Hitler," Kirk recalls. "They won the Second World War."

"Because all this lets them develop the A-bomb first. There's no mistake, Captain. Let me run it again. Edith Keeler. Founder of the peace movement."

"But she was right. Peace was the way."

"She was right, but at the wrong time," Spock replies. "With the A-bomb, and with their V2 rockets to carry them,

---

[2] In "The City on the Edge of Forever", *Star Trek: The Original Series* (S1/E28)

Germany captured the world."

Tracking down Federation historian John Gill on the non-aligned world of Ekos, they discover that he has implemented a fascist world government in the mold of Nazi Germany, with himself as its Fuhrer. Kirk, Spock and McCoy find him in a drugged state, and seek answers.[3]

"Gill. Gill, why did you abandon your mission? Why did you interfere with this culture?" Kirk asks.

"Planet fragmented, divided," Gill mutters in his stupor. "Took lesson from Earth history."

"But why Nazi Germany? You studied history. You knew what the Nazis were!"

"Most efficient state Earth ever knew," Gill replies.

"Quite true, Captain," Spock comments. "That tiny country, beaten, bankrupt, defeated, rose in a few years to stand only one step away from global domination."

"But it was brutal, perverted, had to be destroyed at a terrible cost!"

Something funny is going on within Starfleet. Picard is contacted in very clandestine fashion by a fellow command officer, an old friend, who is clearly disturbed by a series of inexplicable changes at the highest levels of Starfleet Command. Taking this seriously, Picard orders Data to investigate. When his friend's starship explodes shortly thereafter, Data believes it may not have been an accident, based on his investigation:

"My orders were to search for abnormal patterns in Starfleet's directives. I believe I have found just that." He

---

[3] In "Patterns of Force", *Star Trek: The Original Series* (S2/E21)

activates a display.

"These are various outposts and starbases where I have detected unusual activity over the past few months."

"What sort of activity?" Picard asks.

"An uncustomary reshuffling of personnel, usually in the command areas. The new officers have had frequent contact with the highest levels of Starfleet Command."

"Why hasn't anybody discovered this before?"

"The orders were given with great subtlety. To use an aphorism, Starfleet's left hand did not know what its right hand was doing."

"Data, can you speculate as to the purpose of these reassignments?"

"I believe it is a clandestine attempt to control vital sectors of Federation territory."

"This could be a prelude to an invasion," Riker suggests, "but who's behind it?"[4]

A fatal uprising of synths on Mars, which kills tens of thousands, causes a backlash ripple throughout the Federation, aborting a planned attempt to rescue the population of Romulus from an impending supernova. Picard, who would have led the armada, resigns from Starfleet in disgust. In the intervening years, the Federation – and Starfleet in particular – take on an authoritarian tone.[5]

"Why did you quit Starfleet?" a journalist asks him, many years later.

"Because it was no longer Starfleet!" Picard answers

---

[4] In "Conspiracy", *Star Trek: The Next Generation* (S1/E25)

[5] In "Remembrance", *Star Trek: Picard* (S1/E1)

angrily. "We withdrew! The galaxy was mourning, burying its dead, and Starfleet had slunk from its duties!

"The decision to call off the rescue and to abandon those people we had sworn to save was not just dishonorable; it was downright criminal!"

And then there are the Borg, perhaps the ultimate authoritarians, who repeatedly try to assimilate Earth and Starfleet – first, during Picard's early tenure as captain of the *Enterprise*, in which he himself is captured and made Borg[6] – and then again years later, when a Borg cube makes it all the way to Earth again and launches an invasion into Earth's past, to alter history and prevent the Federation from ever forming in the first place.[7]

And decades after *that*, Starfleet is successfully infiltrated by Changeling agents of the Dominion, working in tandem with the Borg, who this time assimilate Picard's own son, Jack – and likewise assimilate all of Starfleet's young officers via a DNA modification introducing Borg biotechnology into their systems via a transporter code infiltration.[8]

Of course, we don't need rising tyranny on Earth or within Starfleet to get the gist of it in Trek; we've always had the ultra-authoritarian Klingon and Romulan empires, and the Cardassian Union, and a lengthy array of others. Authoritarianism and tyranny are alive and well in the 23rd, 24th, and 25th centuries.

We can see, then, that *Trek* has had the threat of authoritarianism and tyranny in its bag of themes from the first season of the first *Trek* to the last season of the latest – and

---

[6] In "The Best of Both Worlds", *Star Trek: The Next Generation* (S3/E26)

[7] In *Star Trek: First Contact*

[8] In *Star Trek: Picard*, S3

offered up many variations on the theme.

Trek demonstrates in allegory what we recall from our actual past and what we observe around us today. The march of authoritarianism and the imposition of tyranny have many paths open to them.

Force. The authoritarian can take control through the use of sheer force – invasion, occupation, assimilation. Kirk and Spock recall this as the route taken by Nazi Germany in "The City on the Edge of Forever" and "Patterns of Force"; it is similarly taken by the Borg in "The Best of Both Worlds" and *Star Trek: First Contact.*

Infiltrating an existing government. The authoritarian can take control, not through force, but by replacing those in government service with their own loyalists – taking an existing governing infrastructure and bending it to their own will, as in the attempted *NextGen* Starfleet coup attempt in "Conspiracy", and the Changeling infiltration of Starfleet in *Picard*, S3.

Othering. The authoritarian tyrant typically distracts a population from its imminent loss of liberty by focusing attention on some group of "others" – people the population can be made to hate, to stir up violent energy and rally them to their new leader. Melakon agitated hatred again Zeon (stand-ins for European Jews) in "Patterns of Force"; the Zhat Vash Romulan cultists managed to inspire hatred of all synthetic life across the Federation population in *Star Trek: Picard.* We see that happening even now in the US, as authoritarianism marches forward; in both the real world and *Trek*, we can find ourselves aghast at the unsettling ease with which these bigotries are summoned.

Grabbing the minds of the young. In *Star Trek: Picard*, Season 3, the Borg Queen manages to capture most of Starfleet by implanting Borg biotechnology in the DNA of young Starfleet officers, bringing them into the collective – and under her control. This is a metaphor for the Hitler Youth, alluded to in "Patterns of Force" and, of course, in our real-world historical record. Though we aren't seeing that kind of indoctrination in the US of the 21st century, we can unfortunately observe a more subtle implantation at work: apathy and disengagement, which accomplishes the same thing.

Ending division through national unity. The aspiring authoritarian tyrant is on the lookout for opportunities, and one of those is a divided population. In "Patterns of Force", Professor John Gill implements a Nazi culture to bring about societal unity, only to have it all go wrong; that same song has been sung in both the Europe and US in the world today (forget that the ones singing are the ones doing the dividing in the first place).

Patterns of force

Studying the encroachment of authoritarian tyranny both today and in decades past, we observe clear patterns. We know what it looks like when a society is forced into autocracy, because the citizens of those societies have reported in full.

Martin Mycielski, Director of Public Affairs of the Open Dialogue Foundation in Brussels, offers a useful summary of what to expect:

- *Fear, lies, a false mandate.* When the authoritarian tyrant walks right through the front door through a democratic process, these will be the primary colors of the palette he uses; it legitimizes his actions, suppresses dissent and resistance, and brings rot into the remnant of the democratic process.
- *A single voice and ideology.* The authoritarian tyrant divides a population through a pretense of unity, presenting his own voice as the one voice of the society he is usurping, putting all who voice their own dissent on the wrong side of the new ideology – to be labeled as unpatriotic (or even

traitors), elitist, or enemies of the state.

- *Seizing the media.* Authoritarian regimes maintain control by taking over the media throughout a society, spreading disinformation and propaganda in a constant stream. China, for instance, censors the Internet, and North Korea doesn't permit access to it at all.
- *Perpetual chaos and anger.* The tyrant distracts a population by stoking anger at straw men or innocents, resulting in chaos that unsettles them which "only they can fix."
- *Distorting the truth.* The constant presentation of lies and disinformation causes perpetual confusion, the result of which will be the erosion of reason in public discourse and its replacement by rising levels of emotion that can be manipulated.
- *Attacks on opposition.* False accusations, scandals, and disinformation about the regime's opponents will become a frequently-deployed tool, not just as domination, but to justify the changing of laws in the regime's favor to suppress the opposition's actions.
- *Limit the freedom to assemble.* One of the most common attacks is on the legal right of the people to assemble; that's where opposition rallies boots-on-the-ground strength, so the authoritarian will use the law to discourage or eliminate that assembly, under the justification of "national security".
- *Attacking the weak.* "Othering", rallying a population against perceived outsiders tagged as threat, is a useful distraction; but another aspect of the practice is to commit egregious wrongs against weaker members of the citizenry – minorities, women – to keep the opposition emotionally

charged, and thereby less effective.

- *Control of the judiciary*. The tyrant will seek to control the courts, to ensure that all legal decisions break in their favor (and against their opposition).
- *Rewriting history*. Authoritarians put great energy and effort into rewriting history in their own favor, distorting the truth about historical or living people who stand against them, and aiming for a new generation of citizens who see the society as they wish for it to be seen, no matter how fabricated that vision might be.
- *Alterations in the electoral system*. Where the authoritarian has not implemented an outright tyranny by force, some electoral system will have elevated them and will still be available to remove them, unless that system changes. This, they will seek to change, insisting that the changes are intended to "correct flaws" in the system

Most of the items on this list – all of which are culled from the experiences of Europeans who have found themselves under authoritarian tyranny – have happened or are happening now in the United States. It will be no surprise to find even more of them in motion as authoritarians take control of the government in the coming years.

Mycielski provides the list above, which he signed "With love, your Eastern European friends", to advise US citizens on what they should be watching for.

Star Trek, of course, gave us many glimpses of this insidious agenda; and the experience of those who have lived through it in the real world, combined with voices like Mycielski's and the other writers quoted below, can not only frame our expectations, but provide us with a plan for response to it when we see it. They are boosting our understanding of what's happening so that we can boost our own capacity to resist it when it does.

JOINING THE AWAY TEAM

Trek's Call to Action

Taking Action

Our *Trek* heroes – from James Kirk to Jean-Luc Picard to Will Riker to Kira Nerys to Worf to Kathryn Janeway to Christopher Pike – are people of action.

They and their peers are indefatigable in their ongoing quests, perpetually focused on making the universe better, one mission at a time – improving themselves, each other, and the lives of any and all they encounter in their travels. They don't shy away from complex challenges, tough decisions, or great risk (risk is, after all, their business!) – they boldly go, even when the risk is daunting and hope is dim.

That's where we are today. The world in this third decade of the 21st century seems overwhelming, as the threats of nationalism, authoritarianism, and even tyranny hover so near. Hope is in short supply, and the risks of standing strong and doing something about it all do indeed seem daunting.

But there is light on our path. Some of it comes from our *Trek* heroes, lessons from their adventures, and some of it comes from experts in our midst. We'll make good use of that light in these pages just ahead, as we consider how we can best equip ourselves for the missions that are coming.

"It's been my experience that the prejudices people feel about each other disappear when they get to know each other."

Break Down Social and Cultural Barriers

Kirk is charged with ferrying a feisty monarch from a powerful family on the planet Elas to the neighboring world of Troyius, where her marriage to one of their leaders will ostensibly bring about peace between the two mutually antagonistic planets.[9]

The Dohlman Elaan is rude, spoiled, bratty, and even violent, and Kirk orders Scotty to take it slow, getting to Troyius, to give him time to prepare her for what is perhaps the ultimate act of diplomacy. He tries to acquaint her with Troyian customs, as a means of acclimating her to the people she will now live among.

"My orders are to take you to Troyius to be married and to see that you learn Troyian customs," he informs her.

"I despise Troyians," she replies. "Any contact with them

---

[9] In "Elaan of Troyius", *Star Trek: The Original Series* (S3/E13)

makes me feel soiled."

"It's been my experience," Kirk counters, "that the prejudices people feel about each other disappear when they get to know each other."

"It's not in my experience."

"Well, we're still faced with the same problem."

"Problem?"

"Yes, the problem of your indoctrination to Troyian customs and manners."

It goes downhill from there, but Kirk's point is all too valid: when we spend time in communities far from our own, among people not at all like us, we almost always take on a broader perception of humanity – and this can't help but erode our prejudices.

"Travel is fatal to prejudice, bigotry, and narrow-mindedness," is how Mark Twain put it, "and many of our people need it sorely on those accounts. Broad, wholesome, charitable views of men and things cannot be acquired by vegetating in one little corner of the earth all one's lifetime."

Saint Augustine said it this way: "The world is a book, and those who do not travel read only one page."

And "He who never leaves his country is full of prejudices," per Carlo Goldoni.

And this particularly poignant observation from Marcel Proust: "The real voyage of discovery consists no in seeking new landscapes, but in having new eyes.

We can take our cue from James Kirk, who certainly understood the power of traveling afar and meeting new people, and consider using travel to faraway places as a means of pushing back prejudices and fortifying our defenses against the autocrat – who would have us forever divided.

Seeing the World

What happens when we get out into the world? What happens when we travel abroad, or even to the far corners of our own country? How do such travels diminish prejudice and bigotry, and expand our minds?

Travel is a powerful tool for dialing down prejudice and bigotry, exposing the traveler to differences in culture and worldview. It is by definition a willful departure from the echo chambers that we often live in at home, where we are surrounded by people who live much as we do and think much as we think.

Seeing how people live in countries and cultures other than our own, or even people living differently in our own country, can be eye-opening in a number of ways:

- **Humanizing Others.** Prejudice and bigotry are emotional reactions to people beyond our social comfort zones that are stoked by those who would divide us – autocrats, oligarchs, religious zealots. The idea is to diminish our inborn empathy for those "Others" by dehumanizing them, characterizing them as less than we are. But when we step into their worlds and observe them, we see that they are much as we are, by no means "less", and as human as any of us. They become individuals, no longer stereotypes. They cease to be "Other", or are at the very least much less "Other", and empathy returns.
- **Expanding Historical Perspective.** When we experience another culture, we are often exposed to that culture's history, which will inevitably differ from our own. That history becomes a window into

how that culture came to be, which bolsters our understanding of the people we're observing and meeting. It puts us on their level, as we understand ourselves by much the same process – where we came from. We may also get glimpses of challenges and injustices that helped shape their point of view, extending our understanding (and empathy) even further.

- **A Global Point of View.** The humanization and historical perspective from another cultural worldview mentioned above serve to instill us with a "global point of view" – an understanding, often elusive to those who live in the isolation of their own backyards, that our corner of the world is just that – a corner. And as we move out into the world, we have an increasing sense that it is, indeed, a world. This, too, extends our understanding of Others as much like us, further bolstering our empathy. People are, on many levels, the same all over, having the same needs, the same desires for happiness, love, family, security, and dignity.

- **Exposure to Different Lifestyles.** We are often convinced by those who would rule over us and divide us that the differences between us and those who live in other places make those people "strange", or that their lifestyles are "wrong" – that their daily practices and traditionss do not conform to the "proper" or "correct" way to live. When we see those practices and traditions for ourselves, and understand how they came to be, we move in the direction of understanding that there really is no "proper" or "correct" way to live, and that the differences are only that – differences. The people we observe are not "strange".

- **Exposure to Different Worldviews.** The autocrat, the oligarch and the religious zealot will all strive to convince us that other differences *are* "strange" and "wrong", even if we accept diversity in lifestyle: the values and beliefs of people in other lands may vary considerably from our own. Yet here, too, when we experience them first-hand and understand their origins, those differing values and beliefs come to make perfect sense – and we can see that they are deeply tied to the identities of those who hold them, as we are to ours.

- **Becoming the Other.** Travel to faraway places can be uncomfortable. Consider that when we are on foreign soil, or even in a far corner of our own country, *we* become the Other – we are the one who doesn't fit in. This forces us to come into confrontation with any prejudices and false assumptions we may be harboring, as those prejudices and assumptions surface in the course of new encounters. That may feel bumpy, but it is an opportunity for growth: we see how they take their own lives for granted, just as we do ours, and must grapple with the realization that our own prejudices and assumptions are actually grounded in ignorance – making us more open.
- **Challenging Narratives.** The false narratives that autocrats propagate to stir up prejudice and bigotry are often successful because they are absurdly simplistic; they seem to offer easily-digested cause-and-effect explanations that are emotionally satisfying (in the area of immigrants, in particular), and have no real factual basis. When we have those narratives challenged by our own first-hand experience, we cannot fail to see that the real world experience of other people in other cultures isn't simple at all; it's deeply and richly complex, and that complexity belies the autocrat's false narrative. We see that what we've been fold about who they

are and how they live bears no resemblance at all to what we've been told.

- **Self-Confrontation.** All of these experiences, all this new information and observation that inevitably accrues when discovering new people in a new place can serve to inspire a process of personal reflection, in which a conscious acknowledgment that how we've seen the people and the place for a long time doesn't reflect who they really and how it really is. In this introspection, a kind of self-confrontation can occur: *What am I going to do with this new information? Should I change my point of view? What can I do with what I've learned, and how can it change the way I engage?* That self-confrontation can also cause us to closely examine our own sense of identity and privilege – *Given that I've been wrong about these people, am I really seeing myself and my own community as we really are, or do I need to make some adjustments there as well?*

- **Getting to Know Each Other.** And, finally, it's not just about our own observations; when we are somewhere else in the world, meeting new people who are part of a different culture, they are observing us as well. The exchanges that happen between us are as informative to them as they are to us, and it can be interesting and revealing to see how they are curious about the same things that make us curious – seeking to understand our values, our traditions, the things that matter to us. In addition to further stimulating our empathy, this can also expand our receptivity to diversity.

"We must find ways to bring people together across social and cultural divides," writes Robert Putnam in his excellent book, *Bowling Along: The Collapse and Revival of American*

Community.

Beyond the Choir

Of course, we're preaching to the choir here. If you're reading this book, you've probably already done the work of excising your prejudices and bad assumptions, and embracing diversity. Diversity, after all, is what *Trek* is all about in the first place. It's likely what attracted you to *Trek*.

The point of this book, however – and the point of this section of the book, in particular – is identifying ways that Trekkers can push back against the rise of authoritarianism in the world today. And the point of this particular chapter is to suggest that, while it's a healthy thing for any of us to visit other countries and get to know people in other cultures, it's of particular value when the experience is undertaken by someone who *does* harbor prejudices, bigotry, and false assumptions.

Do you have family or friends who fall into that category?

Are you in a situation where you could take a vacation abroad, or plan a sabbatical of some kind, and take such a friend or family member with you? It is possible that friend or family member might find themselves won over to a new and better worldview by such an experience? And, if so, would you consider suggesting such an expedition?

If you yourself can't get away, is there merit in encouraging that friend or family member to travel? Are you in a position to persuade them to have an experience that might significantly change their worldview? (You don't have to state your agenda in doing so, of course; it will be good for them if you just make such a suggestion for its own sake.)

At the very least, it is a healthy and positive thing to do for ourselves. Consider taking your next vacation abroad, and make a point of capturing as much of your adventures in sharable format as possible – pics, videos, souvenirs and other artifacts of your experience. Then go out of your way to share them with the friends and family who could do with a little shake-up of their worldview. Tell personal stories about the people you met, what they were like, and the things you did together. Communicate the richness of your experience.

In advancing our embrace of diversity and pushing back against prejudice, even a little helps a lot.

"Mechanically, the computer is flawless. Therefore, logically, its report of the captain's guilt is infallible. I could not accept that, however."

Investigate!

Records Officer Ben Finney is missing from the *Enterprise*, presumed fatally ejected from the ship by Captain Kirk. In the ensuing court martial, the evidence is damning: the ship's computer has logged Kirk's deliberate ejection of the pod under questionable circumstances.[10]

Shortly thereafter, McCoy is stunned to find Spock playing chess on the Rec deck, and chides him for taking a break while the captain's career is at stake. Spock informs him that he's actually doing research; he's beaten the computer at chess repeatedly, which should be impossible, since he himself programmed it for chess. He has established that someone has tampered with the ship's computer – which is relevant

---

[10] In "Court Martial", *Star Trek: The Original Series* (S1/E12)

evidence he will be submitting to Kirk's defense.

Later, McCoy amplifies and then methodically removes the heartbeats of everyone on board the *Enterprise* – leaving one, from an unaccountable source. Finney isn't dead at all; he is still on board, and in hiding.

Find out for yourself!

The authoritarian relies on the masses to accept what they're told – by their own in-group, if not the population as a whole. The autocrat leverages this passive acceptance for his own purposes, and revels in how little effort is often required to sell a belief or an agenda that isn't supported by fact, simply by repeating it often to a group that will then bleat it out.

Never settle for that, not even from your own in-group. Certainly there are people we trust in our lives to inform us honestly and accurately, but it's such a good idea to develop personal investigation as our default, in processing what we learn about events around us.

"Figure things out for yourself," advised Timothy Snyder Spend more time with long articles. Subsidize investigative journalism by subscribing to print media. Realize that some of what is on the Internet is there to harm you. Learn about sites that investigate propaganda campaigns (some of which come from abroad). Take responsibility for what you communicate to others."

"'What is truth?' he goes on to ask. "Sometimes people ask this question because they wish to do nothing. Generic cynicism makes us feel hip and alternative even as we slip along with our fellow citizens into a morass of indifference. It is your ability to discern facts that makes you an individual, and our collective trust in common knowledge that makes us a society. The individual who investigates is also the citizen who builds. The leader who dislikes the investigators is a potential tyrant.

"If we do pursue the facts, the internet gives us enviable power to convey them. Leszek Kołakowski, the great Polish philosopher and historian, lost his chair at Warsaw University for speaking out against the communist regime, and could not publish. The first quotation in this book, from Hannah Arendt, came from a pamphlet entitled 'We Refugees', a miraculous achievement written by someone who had escaped a murderous Nazi regime. A brilliant mind like Victor Klemperer, much admired today, is remembered only because he stubbornly kept a hidden diary under Nazi rule. For him it was sustenance: 'My diary was my balancing pole, without which I would have fallen down a thousand times.'

He quotes others on the topic:

"If the main pillar of the system is living a lie," wrote Václav Havel, "then it is not surprising that the fundamental threat to it is living in truth."[11] Synder added, "Since in the age of the internet we are all publishers, each of us bears some private responsibility for the public's sense of truth. If we are serious about seeking the facts, we can each make a small revolution in the way the internet works. If you are verifying information for yourself, you will not send on fake news to others. If you choose to follow reporters whom you have reason to trust, you can also transmit what they have learned to others. If you retweet only the work of humans who have followed journalistic protocols, you are less likely to debase your brain interacting with bots and trolls. We do not see the minds that we hurt when we publish falsehoods, but that does not mean we do no harm."

And Hanna Arendt:

""Under normal circumstances the liar is defeated by reality, for which there is no substitute; no matter how large the tissue of falsehood that an experienced liar has to offer, it will never be large enough, even if he enlists the help of computers, to cover the immensity of factuality." ...to which Snyder added, "The part about computers is no longer true. For many Americans, the two-dimensional world of the internet has

---

[11] In the essay "The Power of the Powerless".

become more important than the three-dimensional world of human contact. People going door-to-door encounter the surprised blinking of American citizens who realize that they have to talk about politics with a flesh-and-blood human being rather than having their views affirmed by their Facebook feeds. Within the two-dimensional internet world, new collectivities have arisen, invisible by the light of day - tribes with distinct worldviews, beholden to manipulations."

Still, Arendt was making an important point about "the inherent power of facts to overcome falsehoods in a free society."

Spock was not content to accept facts that felt incoherent – even when they came from the ship's computer. So he investigated; he found out for himself. He and McCoy pursued the real facts with boots-on-the-ground diligence.

Do the same; arm yourself with facts, and gather them yourself.

"They want us to lose our heads!"

Remain Calm

Kirk's *Enterprise* is beyond the boundaries of Federation space on a star-mapping mission, intimidated by the arrival of a vast starship hundreds of times its own size – captained by an alien named Balok who declares that the *Enterprise* has transgressed by violating his race's borders. Their punishment will be death.[12]

Lieutenant Bailey, new to the bridge, is losing it.

"I don't understand this!" he suddenly declares. "Spock's wasting time! Everybody else just sitting around... somebody's got to do something!"

"Easy, Bailey," McCoy counsels.

"What do they want from us? Let's find out what they want us to do!"

"They want us to lose our heads," Kirk says levelly – and accurately.

In the end, Balok's behavior wasn't authoritarian at all; he

---

[12] In "The Corbomite Manuever", *Star Trek: The Original Series* (S1/E10)

was, in fact, quite benign, and was simply learn who the people of Starfleet and the Federation really were. But his tactics – his attempts to intimidate, to spark fear, to pressure the *Enterprise* crew into panicked self-disclosures – are right out of the authoritarian playbook.

"Be calm when the unthinkable arrives," Timothy Snyder warned. "Modern tyranny is terror management. When the terrorist attack comes, remember that authoritarians exploit such events in order to consolidate power. The sudden disaster that requires the end of checks and balances, the dissolution of opposition parties, the suspension of freedom of expression, the right to a fair trial, and so on, is the oldest trick in the Hitlerian book. *Do not fall for it.*"

He also noted that no less than Framer James Madison advocated active response to such terror tactics, particularly in precarious circumstances:

"James Madison nicely made the point that tyranny arises 'on some favorable emergency.' After the Reichstag fire, Hannah Arendt wrote that 'I was no longer of the opinion that one can simply be a bystander.' One coup has been attempted. A failed coup is usually practice for a successful one. The emergency might be more favorable next time, and we cannot afford to be surprised."

Mycielski pointed out that one way the authoritarian tries to get us to lose our heads, in Kirk's words, is by striking at innocents whose violation will provoke our response:

"When invading your liberal sensibilities, they will focus on what hurts the most – women and minorities," he wrote. "They will act as if democracy was majority rule without respect for the minority. They will paint foreigners and immigrants as potential threats. Racial, religious, sexual and other minorities will become enemies to the order and security they are supposedly providing. They will challenge women's social status, undermine gender equality and interfere with reproductive rights. But it means they are aware of the threat women and minorities pose to their rule, so make it your strength.

"Women and minorities have to be ready to fight the hardest – reminding the majority what true democracy is about – and you must fight together with them."

Kirk has it right – they want us to lose our heads. And his prescription is the same as Snyder's – *remain calm*. The unthinkable *will* arrive, and there's no use kidding ourselves about it. The authoritarian does the unthinkable *precisely for that reason* – to push us into freaking out the way Bailey did.

Don't fall for it. Remain at your post, and get out the corbomite...

"We shall always retain the best part of the other inside us."

Have a Support System

Picard's *Enterprise* will oversee initial negotiations with a new race, the Legarans, to be conducted by the Vulcan Ambassador Sarek — Spock's father. The mission is complicated by the fact that Sarek has Bendii Syndrome, a rare disorder that causes elderly Vulcans to lose control of their emotions and experience irrational anger. Picard is alarmed at this obvious threat to the success of their mission, but both Sarek and his wife Perrin deny that he is ill.[13]

Sarek's aide Sakkath, also a Vulcan, has secretly been providing the ambassador with telepathic support to help him maintain emotional control. Perrin and Mendrossen, Sarek's chief of staff, have been carefully isolating him, so that "he could complete this one last task and end his career with dignity," Perrin explains to Picard.

And then Picard, with Beverly's help, goes the extra mile in lending his support to this group effort: he agrees to a mind

---

[13] In "Sarek", *Star Trek: The Next Generation* (S3/E23)

meld with Sarek that will allow him to carry the burdens of Sarek's emotions while Sarek meets with the Legarans, fortified with Picard's emotional control and diplomatic skills.

Sarek's support system sustained him through a very difficult political challenge, and it was two-fold; one, providing dignity and strength, while the second provided functional support to accomplish the mission.

Trek provides many such examples, and their takeaway is this: when facing adversity, we need a support system that will have this same two-fold nature. It needs to give us strength and inner resources, while also bolstering our ability to act.

We have seen, above, several examples of the first – cultivating community, pushing back against isolation and loneliness, promoting civility, embracing diversity, being mindful of focused human contact, breaching cultural barriers – all of these provide strength to us and those we work with, as well as a vast array of supporting emotional resources.

And we know that investigation, advocacy for truth, giving to causes that matter, improving our use of language, proactivity, practicing civil disobedience, defending our institutions, and enforcing privacy all serve our mission.

We need to build up groups around us of people who will support us in these ways – and whom we can support in turn. An individual fighting the authoritarian is easily dispatched; a committed group of allies, not so much. There are no Away Teams of one.

We need to seek out the Perrins and Sakkaths and Mendrossens who will stand strong with us, building that strength through community and human contact; defending dignity through civility and inclusion, pushing through cultural divides.

And we need the Picards and Crushers, who will bond with us as we do the work – showing up, investigating, defending those things that need defending, speaking the truth, speaking out against bad laws, rising up in peaceful protest.

The convenient aspect of this support system building is that it happens through exactly these actions.

Educating yourself about issues at the local level will inform you about who stands where on those issues. You can see who needs your support. Cultivating community brings you into contact with those who have something to offer you and to whom you in turn can offer support. Across cultural and geographic divides, you'll find more allies still, diverse ones with fresh viewpoints and backgrounds that will inform you. And the sharpening skill of eye contact and enhanced attention in personal interaction will help you sense who you can trust and who you can't.

As these relationships develop, you can enter into privacy agreements with your companions, reinforcing good personal data hygiene. The same applies to mindfulness of language – both the dog whistles of the authoritarian and his followers, and your own renewed ability to frame. Discuss that framing, and those dog whistles, with your team.

Like most aspects of resistance, this one will vary a great deal, person to person. Your support system will be just that – yours. Unlike any others. The trick is to do a better job of it than Sarek did; don't convince yourself you can do it all on your own. Find your Perrins. Find your Picards!

*"Revisionist history:
it's such a comfort!"*

Be Well-Informed

In the Delta Quadrant, the Kyrians have a museum on their world dedicated to *Voyager*'s savage attack on their planet 700 years in the past, in which tens of thousands of Kyrians were killed. The attack was, they believe, in support of the aggression of their neighbors, the Vaskans. Relics from *Voyager* – including a photon torpedo and a tricorder – adorn a wing of the museum just outside a simulation room, where decks of *Voyager* have been recreated and scenes from the prelude to the massacre may be viewed.

A Kyrian historian presides over the museum, sharing with visitors the story of *Voyager*'s heinous attacks on their planet. He earnestly believes the history he is sharing, which is challenged when a backup module of *Voyager*'s holographic Doctor is discovered. He activates the Doctor, who is mortified by the horrific inaccuracy of the Kyrian recreation of *Voyager*'s long-ago visit to their world – including his own profile as a mass murderer.[14]

He painstakingly sets the record straight, generating a more accurate simulation of what Janeway and his other colleagues actually said and did when meeting with the Kyrians and Vaskans who came aboard *Voyager*.

"You're lying!" the historian accuses him.

"I was there!" the Doctor replies.

"You're trying to protect yourself."

"And so are you! From the truth! Isn't it a coincidence that the Kyrians are being portrayed in the best possible light? Martyrs, heroes, saviors. Obviously, events have been reinterpreted to make your people feel better about themselves. Revisionist history. It's such a comfort!"

After some soul-searching, the historian realizes he must be open to revising his thinking about what really happened. Meanwhile, protest and violence erupt between the Kyrians and the Vaskans living in the planet over the Doctor's testimony, disrupting their uneasy peace and threatening terrible escalation. The historian decides that the truth has priority – and he helps the Doctor produce evidence, from the tricorder, that his version of history is the accurate one.

The Doctor's experience is all too common, isn't it? The cliché that "history is written by the winners" presents over and over again in our own. And the revisionists are, invariably, the winning autocrats: egalitarians understand history as collective heritage, prefer to base their future decisions on the trial-and-error learnings of the past – good and bad – and have no interest in living in lies.

"The belief that an informed citizenry is essential to the survival of American democracy is as old as the republic itself,"

---

wrote Richard Haass. "Thomas Jefferson emphasized the link, pointing out that 'wherever the people are well informed they can be trusted with their own government; that whenever things get so far wrong as to attract their notice, they may be relied on to set them to rights.' Some two centuries later, the forty-fourth president, Barack Obama, made a similar point, arguing that 'This democracy doesn't work if we don't have an informed citizenry.'"

The admonitions of Jefferson and Obama notwithstanding, the US has been by no means exempt from the consequences of poorly-informed citizens. Efforts by those who insist on being well-informed, and helping others to be as well, can rise to the level of the heroic.

A relatively recently example in the American story is the story of Daniel Ellsberg, a journalist and analyst who, after eyewitnessing the escalating conflict in Vietnam in the Sixties, photocopied secure documents locked away at the RAND Corporation, where he later worked. The documents were massive reports compiled by Robert McNamara, former Secretary of Defense under Presidents Kennedy and Johnson, summarizing the true history of the Vietnam conflict. They documented extensive falsehoods foisted upon the American public by half a dozen presidential administrations, including those of Kennedy, Johnson, and Nixon; the war was, in fact, hopeless, they had known it for years, and president after president kept sending American boys to die anyway.

Ellsberg, having seen this for himself, decided the public needed to be as well-informed as he was; so he leaked the documents, which came to be known as the Pentagon Papers, to journalist Neil Sheehan of the *New York Times*. The *Times* and the *Washington Post* published them for all to see, inspiring rage in the Nixon White House, triggering a Supreme Court showdown – and bringing tremendous persecution to Ellsberg's doorstep.

It was the right thing to do, and it caused great furor – but it also changed the course of American history. Public outcry led to the long-overdue cessation of US military action in Vietnam.

"Why is an informed citizenry essential?" Haass asked. "American democracy is a representative (rather than direct) democracy, in which citizens do not make day-to-day decisions as to what the federal, state, or local government should do with its powers and resources but rather elect individuals to do just that. It is thus a republic; in the words of James Madison, 'a government which derives all its powers directly or indirectly from the great body of the people, and is administered by persons holding their offices during pleasure, for a limited period, or during good behavior.' The obvious reason, then, for citizens to be informed is to be able to wisely cast their votes. In almost every instance there are two or more candidates vying for a position, and it is in your self-interest to know enough to determine which of the candidates would be likely to advance or support policies you judge to be desirable. Implicit in this decision is knowing not simply what a candidate stands for but also the likely consequences of the policies they stand for and oppose so that you are in a position to determine what policy choices make the most sense."

Be the Doctor. Be a living witness; dig up evidence, put it on the table - and raise up your voice, whenever you must, to set the record straight.

"I wish it were as easy to stop hating as it was to start."

Make Smart Use of Language

Commander Chakotay's shuttle crashes on a Delta quadrant world where a vicious war has long been waged, and he finds himself among the Vori, one of the two warring nations. Through the very targeted use of language and with heightened emotional stimulation, they manage to brainwash him into adopting their worldview and embracing their cause, becoming one of their soldiers.[15]

Tuvok rescues him, and the Doctor explains what was done to him.

"From the condition of your hypothalamus, I'd say they had you so mixed up they could have convinced you your own mother was a turnip," the Doctor comments.

"Everything I experienced was some sort of simulation?"

"The idea was to make you bond with your fellow soldiers as well as the villagers, so their deaths would enrage you,"

---

[15] In "Nemesis", *Star Trek: Voyager* (S4/E4)

Captain Janeway adds.

"In short, Commander, you've been subjected to a highly sophisticated form of propaganda," the Doctor says.

"I cared about the Vori, but I hated the Kradin," Chakotay admits. "I wanted to kill every one of them."

"Evidently, that was the point."

When Archer's *Enterprise* diverts to a planet hosting a Vulcan monastery, he is surprised to discover hostile Andorians there, accusing the Vulcan elders there of hiding a long-range sensor array there, to be used to spy on them. The presence of a Starfleet vessel at the monastery boosts their suspicions.[16]

Archer is interrogated, and he does his best to explain his presence and to defend the elders. But as dialog degenerates into violence, it's discovered that there in the mists of conflicting cultural subtext is an awkward truth: the Andorians are right, and the Vulcans do indeed have a long-range sensor array, and are indeed lying about it.

Making contact with a Tamarian ship at El-Adrel, Picard finds himself transported to the planet's surface along with the other ship's captain, Dathon. The Federation has never been able to make any headway with the Tamarians, as their language is built on narrative metaphor; constant allusions to their culture's history and mythology are how they communicate with one another. The universal translator,

---

[16] In "The Andorian Incident", *Enterprise* (S1/E7)

then, is useless.[17]

Aboard the *Enterprise*, Riker, Troi and the other senior officers work on the language barrier issue:

"The Tamarian ego structure does not seem to allow what we normally think of as self-identity," Data tells the others. "Their ability to abstract is highly unusual. They seem to communicate through narrative imagery by reference to the individuals and places which appear in their mytho-historical accounts."

"It's as if I were to say to you, 'Juliet on her balcony,'" Troi adds.

"An image of romance," Crusher nods.

"Exactly. Imagery is everything to the Tamarians. It embodies their emotional states, their very thought processes. It's how they communicate, and it's how they think."

"If I didn't know who Juliet was or what she was doing on that balcony, the image alone wouldn't have any meaning."

On the planet below, Picard and Dathon find themselves battling a deadly predator and are unable to beam back to their respective vessels. Picard realizes that Dathon is trying to express a strategy for battle the beast through allegory, and begins to understand that Dathon's idea is based on a story of a previous battle between two Tamarian warriors and a similar beast. Picard responds in kind, sharing some of the *Epic of Gilgamesh*. Eventually he understands that Dathon has been trying to make a diplomatic overture, offering friendship in the face of shared danger, as in the story he wishes to share.

Dathon does not survive, but Picard is able to vanquish the beast in the end. Back aboard the *Enterprise*, he reaches out

---

[17] In "Darmok", *Star Trek: The Next Generation* (S5/E2)

to Dathon's second-in-command on the other ship, offering Dathon's diary and dagger. He is told to keep them in remembrance of Dathon's sacrifice, which has forged a bond between their two peoples. Their own contribution will be a new addition to their language: the phrase, "Picard and Dathon at El-Adrel! Mirab, with sails unfurled!"

Lots going on here, and all of it deeply relevant to the threat of authoritarianism.

First is the issue of *framing* – exploiting words and phrases to control public discourse by crafting a context around them that triggers certain ideas in the mind of the listener.

Then there's the conscious mobilization of language itself to usurp social and cultural control. The US political right has been doing this for decades.

Finally, the authoritarian uses a particular set of words that are giveaways, if we know to listen for them.

Let's look at each of these.

Use your words!

Early in my cognitive psychology studies, I came across George Lakoff.

The first book I read by the Berkley language expert was *Metaphors We Live By*, which suggested that we build our internal models of the world out of frameworks driven by concepts about reality that we've absorbed, and expand our understanding by assigning meaning sitting in one frame to the new frames we build.

Put another way, when I hear or experience something new, I will subconsciously push toward an understanding of it by

dropping it into a frame I already possess.
Example:

Argument is war

This metaphor takes the concept of *argument* and drops it into the *war* frame I possess. If I take this metaphor on board, then I will assign the features of *war* to my understanding of *argument*: war is conflict; there is a winner and a loser; the idea is to defeat the other person. Argument, in this metaphor, becomes conflict, and the objective is to defeat the other.
Then again:

Argument is dance

This metaphor works the same way, but in assigning a different frame, it imbues *argument* with different features: when two people dance, there is move and countermove; there is cooperation; there is synchronization, in varying degrees; and there is a shared goal. Viewed within the *dance* frame, *argument* becomes altogether different.
Lakoff isn't just a language expert; he's also a political activist, authoring *The Political Mind* and *Don't Think of an Elephant!*, two books that bring this framing concept into the realm of politics, where it is leveraged to high heaven. Political rhetoric oozes framing language, and it is used to steer our thinking without our realizing it.☐
Example, from Lakoff:

"Take "tax relief," a phrase used by the current White House [Bush II]. The word *relief* evokes a conceptual frame of some affliction - an afflicted party, and a reliever who performs the action of relieving. So taxes are an affliction, a reliever is a hero, and anyone who wants to stop him from the relief is a villain. You have just two words, yet all of that is embedded. If you oppose reducing taxes and you use that phrase - *tax relief* -

you've already lost."

Put another way,

"For there to be relief, there must be an affliction, an afflicted party, and a reliever who removes the affliction and is therefore a hero. And if people try to stop the hero, those people are villains for trying to prevent relief. When the word tax is added to relief, the result is a metaphor: Taxation is an affliction. And the person who takes it away is a hero, and anyone who tries to stop him is a bad guy. This is a frame. It is made up of ideas, like affliction and hero."

And here's another Lakoff example quoting Bush II:

Another example Lakoff mentions in his book is when Bush proclaimed in his State of the Union address in January 2005 that "we do not need a permission slip to defend America." Consider what Bush is saying here. Sure, he could have said, "we won't ask permission," but saying "permission slip" evokes the adult-child metaphor, which aligns with conservatives' strict father worldview, according to Lakoff.

The Republicans weren't always so savvy about framing. Lakoff is fond of pointing out that when Nixon got on television and stated, *I am not a crook!*", he was foolishly invoking a frame that doomed him: now Americans could see him as nothing *but* a crook.

In the years since, Republicans have come to understand framing thoroughly; they not only actively practice it incessantly (for decades now), but write playbooks about it.

Newt Gingrich, for instance, when planning his conservative resurgence in Congress in the early Nineties, he wrote a memo that was distributed to Republican officeholders entitled "Language: A Key Mechanism of Control".

"In it, he carried on from Joseph Goebbels, who had

repeatedly asserted that in order to control a society, one must first take control of that society's language. Gingrich gave Republicans a list of words to describe anything having to do with Democrats," wrote Thom Hartmann in *The Hidden History of American Oligarchy*:

decay, failure (fail), collapse(ing), deeper, crisis, urgent(cy), destructive, destroy, sick, pathetic, lie, liberal, they/them, unionized bureaucracy, "compassion" is not enough, betray, consequences, limit(s), shallow, traitors, sensationalists, endanger, coercion, hypocrisy, radical, threaten, devour, waste, corruption, incompetent, permissive attitude, destructive, impose, self-serving, greed, ideological, insecure, anti-(issue): flag, family, child, jobs; pessimistic, excuses, intolerant, stagnation, welfare, corrupt, selfish, insensitive, status quo, mandate(s) taxes, spend (ing) shame, disgrace, punish (poor . . .), bizarre, cynicism, cheat, steal, abuse of power, machine, bosses, obsolete, criminal rights, red tape, patronage.

"Gingrich told Republicans that it was as important to characterize themselves in a positive light as it was to trash-talk Democrats. His list of words to apply to themselves and their policies was as follows," Hartmann continued:

share, change, opportunity, legacy, challenge, control, truth, moral, courage, reform, prosperity, crusade, movement, children, family, debate, compete, active(ly), we/us/our, candid(ly), humane, pristine, provide, liberty, commitment, principle(d), unique, duty, precious, premise, care(ing), tough, listen, learn, help, lead, vision, success, empower(ment), citizen, activist, mobilize, conflict, light, dream, freedom, peace, rights, pioneer, proud/pride, building, preserve, pro-(issue): flag, children, environment; reform, workfare, eliminate good-time in prison, strength, choice/choose, fair, protect, confident, incentive, hard work, initiative, common sense, passionate.

"When tyranny begins to emerge, shifts in language become obvious, and it's important to pay close attention to how language is used, especially when certain phrases or memes are used repeatedly," Hartmann wrote. "Tyrants understand that it's more important to control the news than to control the army; armies will follow what they believe to be true, but only when first convinced of its truth, and that requires control of or substantial influence over the news."

So blatant is this manipulative usage that it is now a standard practice among Republican lawmakers to simply name things the opposite of what they really are, in order to have them accepted: *The Clear Skies Initiative! No Child Left Behind!*

Both Lakoff and Hartmann have spent years trying to get Democratic leaders to take this message seriously and to realize that they are only hurting themselves by submitting to the framing used by their opponents, rather than developing their own.

Bill Clinton was the exception, Lakoff noted: he understood framing and how to make it work, not just for him, but against his opposition.

"He stole the other side's language," Lakoff wrote. "He walked about 'welfare reform', for example. He said, 'The age of big government is over.' He did what he wanted to do, only he took their language and used their words to describe it. It made them very mad."

Overtures to both the Obama team and Hillary Clinton team were dismissed, Lakoff has lamented. Either the psychology itself wasn't being taken seriously, or the use of framing as a method of political persuasion was being interpreted as manipulation.

But is it? Doesn't every effective speechwriter, regardless of their political leaning, employ exactly these techniques? Didn't Lincoln? Didn't JFK and King? Framing is simply science; it's how human brains work. Is it out-of-bounds to employ it inaccurately get one's message across?

Lakoff summarizes frames as "mental structures that shape the way we see the world." They are neither left nor right; they're simply there. And we are all carrying around many frames, often covering the same domain; it isn't manipulation to take care to use words that steer your message into the frame you intend. It's stupid, in fact, not to.

A final point, this one from Hartmann: liberals try to engage the mind, while conservatives try to engage emotions; liberals talk facts, conservatives tell stories. The intuitive advantage of the conservative messaging is that human brains become emotionally engaged first, intellectually engaged thereafter; and the human brain's ancient roots are in storytelling, while recitation of fact is relatively new in history. Liberals, then, are employing a losing strategy when they fail to learn from how conservatives communicate.

It's not tough to learn these principles and commit to them; and it's long past time the left got its act together, and started truly using their words.

What to listen for

From Snyder: "Victor Klemperer, a literary scholar of Jewish origin, turned his philological training against Nazi propaganda. He noticed how Hitler's language rejected legitimate opposition: The people always meant some people and not others (an American president said my people), encounters were always struggles (an American variant is winning), and any attempt to understand the world in a different way was defamation of the leader (or, as an American president put it, treason).

"Politicians in our times feed their clichés to television, where even those who wish to disagree repeat them. Television purports to challenge political language by conveying images, but the succession from one frame to another can hinder a sense of resolution. Everything happens fast, but nothing actually happens. Each story on televised news is "breaking" until it is displaced by the next one. So we are hit by wave upon wave but never see the ocean."

"Listen for dangerous words," Snyder went on to advise: "Be alert to the use of the words *extremism* and *terrorism*. Be alive to the fatal notions of *emergency* and *exception*. Be angry about the treacherous use of patriotic vocabulary."

And from Mycielski:

"They will distort the language, coin new terms and labels, repeat shocking phrases until you accept them as normal and subconsciously associate them with whom they like. A "thief", "liar" or "traitor" will automatically mean the opposition, while a "patriot" or a "true American" will mean their follower (see point 2). Their slogans will have double meaning, giving strength to their supporters and instilling angst in their opponents. *Fight changes in language in the public sphere, remind and preserve the true meaning of words.*"

Finally, there's the lesson of El-Adrel: it's not enough to share words themselves with those we bond with as allies; we must go the extra mile in learning their stories, and getting to what those stories mean to them – and sharing our own.

"And they got all this from watching Damar's speech?"

Protect Your Privacy

Four genetic augments are being studied by Dr. Bashir on *Deep Space Nine*, who notes that they are all highly intelligent but that their augmentation has imposed side effects that limit their usefulness in Federation society. One is paranoid, one is childlike, one is hypersexual, and one is silent. And Federation law, being quite rigid when it comes to genetic engineering, excludes them from professions where their augmented intelligence could be put to work.[18]

Bored, they study a speech by Damar, the new leader of the Cardassians, who is suggesting peace talks between his people and the Federation. They are able to extract subtle clues from Damar's phrasing and behavior which indicate that he wants the border modified to give the Cardassians access to a planet with the raw materials for the drug ketracel white, which is used to control the Jem'Hadar soldiers of the Dominion. This obviously is a big help to the Federation's

---

[18] In "Statistical Probabilities", *Star Trek: Deep Space Nine* (S6/E9)

negotiators.

Starfleet boosts the intelligence of the augments further, enabling them to develop a predictive model that foretells the Federation's defeat by the Dominion, costing hundreds of billions of Federation lives. They recommend surrender, which both Sisko and Starfleet reject. The augments then try to leak Starfleet's strategic plans to the Dominion in order to hasten the Federation's defeat with minimal loss of life. Bashir manages to stop them, and they are returned to forced isolation.

Privacy is one of the greatest issues and challenges we face, rising authoritarianism aside. In the age of the cell phone, Internet, social media, and machine learning, it's difficult to know where to even start in considering and addressing how threats to our privacy affect us – let alone what we should do about them.

When we add authoritarianism to the mix, seeing how our personal information can be turned against us, the issue feels openly oppressive.

"What the great political thinker Hannah Arendt meant by totalitarianism was not an all-powerful state, but the erasure of the difference between private and public life," wrote Timothy Synder. "We are free only insofar as we exercise control over what people know about us, and in what circumstances they come to know it."

Our personal privacy can be violated in a number of ways that compromise our well-being and safety, both individually and collectively:

- **Personal ID information.** Too much identifying information makes us easier to track and hack.
- **Health information.** Information about our personal health or health history can be exploited

to our financial and career disadvantage. That's why HIPAA regulations are in place today, and why deregulating personal health information would be desirable to the authoritarian.

- **Ethnicity and sexuality.** Disclosure of personal details about our ethnicity and sexual orientation can be used to have us targeted for discrimination, or even make us sought out by hate groups.
- **Social media expression.** Many if not most of us express ourselves regularly on social media, and reveal details about our lives, our opinions, our backgrounds. All of this information is exploitable, in the wrong hands.
- **Harvested self-expression in machine learning.** That same social media data, as well as more private information (such as health and financial records) can – even if anonymous – be bundled with the data of thousands of other people and folded into machine learning processes, creating powerful and unregulated AI, which can be used for a broad array of dark purposes useful to the authoritarian.

"Nastier rulers will use what they know about you to push you around," wrote Timothy Snyder. "If we have no control over who reads what and when, we have no ability to act in the present or plan for the future. Whoever can pierce your privacy can humiliate you and disrupt your relationships at will. No one (except perhaps a tyrant) has a private life that can survive public exposure by hostile directive."

The uncomfortable truth is that most of us are pretty free and easy with our online lives. We leave big trails of private information behind us wherever we go in cyberspace, and essentially fill out exhaustively detailed profiles of ourselves as we go – profiles that are easily accessed by those who know how. The more information about ourselves we exude, the more vulnerable we are to threat or manipulation by the authoritarian. And we can do something about that.

Buttoning Up Our Lives

By taking very deliberate steps to protect our personal privacy, and by encouraging our friends and family members to do the same, we take a giant step back from the encroaching autocrat. We make it that much harder for they to control us, to exploit us, to threaten us. We are safer; they are spread more thinly, the more of us there are who take such steps.

Here are some of those steps:

- **Passwords.** Take password security *very* seriously; hacking in this domain has become deeply sophisticated. Many sites and apps require highly complex passwords. Go with it.[19]
- **Two-factor authentication.** Having to authenticate twice rather than once to open an app or gain access to a web page is a pain, it's true; but adding a spontaneously-generated access code to a password requirement doesn't just double the security – it bumps it up exponentially.
- **Public wi-fi.** There are few environments more unsafe than public wi-fi. Those who make use of public wi-fi, even just to check email, are running a big risk of having their laptop or tablet compromised, offering access to account information, etc. Public wi-fi should only be used for the most innocuous purposes, when other security measures are in place to protect

---

[19] This seems intimidating at times, but can be fun; for instance, you can create a password from a phrase you'll never forget: **Tbgw-1hgb4!** ("To boldly go where no one has gone before!"

information on the device being used.

- **Anti-virus software.** Use it, make sure it's high-quality, and make sure you take the updates, as improvements address the latest threats.
- **Privacy settings on apps and websites.** Many apps and websites offer the user control over what data may and may not be shared. Take the time to review these options when they are offered, and make prudent choices.
- **Cookies and other browser trackers.** Many if not most companies want to put cookies on your device. This allows them to track your activity, not just when using their apps and visiting their sites, but to map your trail to other sites. They do this in order to create buying behavioral analytics. Profitable for them, potentially invasive for you.
- **Do personal in person.** It's a wise policy, not just with regard to online habits but in life generally, to have personal exchanges in person. Safer, from a privacy standpoint, and healthier, from a human one.
- **Need to know.** Don't self-disclose casually on social media unless the subject matter is innocuous (football team biases, etc.). Only put information online that others really need to know. Get in the habit of asking yourself before hitting Enter.
- **Learn about online scams.** There are many effective scams in play, all over the digital universe. Many are email-related, intending to bait the user into giving up hackable knowledge. Learn what these are and how to avoid them.
- **Private web browser.** Just as cookies planted in your machine make your online activity

trackable, so some browsers track your activity for marketing and ad-targeting purposes. But your digital footprints also reveal other information about you, so it's best to leave no trail at all. Consider a private web browser like DuckDuckGo or Ecosia.

- **Opt-out on demographic details.** Many online forms and questionnaires provide users with the option of omitting various demographic details about themselves. It's a good default to opt out of any revelation of demographic detail that doesn't strike you as essential.

The authoritarian threats made possible through privacy invasions are serious, even potentially grave, Snyder warned.

"Scrub your computer of malware on a regular basis," he advised. "Remember that email is skywriting. Consider using alternative forms of the internet, or simply using it less. Have personal exchanges in person. For the same reason, resolve any legal trouble. Tyrants seek the hook on which to hang you. Try not to have hooks."

"Your heart is Klingon; it will be done!"

Embrace and promote civility

Kirk's *Enterprise* is en route to the neutral planetoid Babel with more than 100 diplomats aboard from many Federation worlds, on their way to debate the question of whether to admit Coridan to the union.[20]

Tensions are running high, as the question is a controversial one. And the races represented in the reception held in the *Enterprise* lounge are not altogether harmonious in their interactions. But Kirk, Spock and McCoy set a polite example, offering calming answers to snippy questions.

The same can be said of Ambassador Sarek, Spock's father, who is accosted by a drunk Tellarite over his reticence to speak of the Vulcan government's position on the Coridan question. Civility, not confrontation, is the active choice, even when bad tempers flare.

Worf faces family dishonor when the Klingon High Council accepts an accusation that his father committed treason – a lie – for political purposes. He is discommodated – cast out –

---

[20] In "Journey to Babel", *Star Trek: The Original Series* (S2/E10)

an utter humiliation for a shame he should not have to bear.

He has every right to face his accuser in mortal combat and fight for his family's honor. But he makes a different choice, one that earns him the admiration of his captain and fellow officers; he accepts the unjust rejection with quiet dignity, remaining respectful to a council that includes dishonest antagonists, and through his civility demonstrates magnificent strength and character.[21]

"Civility and being civil to others are essential to the workings of democracy. Civility is closely aligned with manners. With respect. With courtesy. With politeness," wrote Richard Haass. "To learn how to disagree without being disagreeable. To paraphrase the Golden Rule, civility is about treating others as you would like others to treat you.

"At least two former presidents have weighed in on the word," he continued. "John F. Kennedy, in his famous 'Ask not what your country can do for you - ask what you can do for your country' inaugural address, noted that 'civility is not a sign of weakness.' Forty years later, in his first inaugural address, George W. Bush expressed it this way: 'Civility is not a tactic or a sentiment; it is the determined choice of trust over cynicism, of community over chaos.' Why is this concept so important? Disagreements are inevitable in a democracy. Opinions often are strong or even emotional. The subject can be anything, be it public spending, taxes, race, gender, political and personal rights, abortion, guns, masks, vaccinations, arrangements for voting or the counting of ballots, or matters of war and peace. What civility does is make it possible for differences to be reduced or even bridged - and even if not, civility allows for dialogue and relationships to continue on other issues where

---

[21] In "Sins of the Father", *Star Trek: The Next Generation* (S3/E17)

agreement might not be out of the question. Opponents on one issue need not become opponents on all issues, much less enemies. Civility greatly decreases the chances that disagreements will spill over into violence. How can civility be promoted? It is best to deal with issues and arguments on their merits, not on motives you might ascribe to those making the arguments."

Our heroes model that strength and character in the face of adversity through their commitment to civility, even when – as in Worf's case – the adversity is demeaning, humiliating. The strength and character derive from the willingness to remain committed to civility even at great personal cost – prioritizing humanity-affirming traits that strengthen us all over self-interest, even self-defense.

"If you really are interested in small talk, then you should keep your eye on Commander Hutchinson at the reception this afternoon.
He's a master!"

On the Importance of Small Talk and Eye Contact

Picard's *Enterprise* has arrived at a starbase at the planet Arkaria for some ship maintenance. The bridge staff is looking forward, more or less, to a reception to be given in their honor by the base commander. Data steps onto a turbolift already occupied by Captain Picard.[22]

"It has been quite a day, has it not?" Data unexpectedly asks.

Picard, a little surprised, nods.

"Yes, it has."

"However, change of routine is often invigorating and can

---

be a welcome diversion after a long assignment."

Picard doesn't know what to say to that, so he just says, "Exactly."

"I understand that Arkaria has some very interesting weather patterns."

At this point Data is so out of character that Picard can't help but ask, "Mister Data, are you all right?"

"Yes, sir," Data replies. "I am attempting to fill a silent moment with non-relevant conversation."

Now Picard understands. He nods. "Small talk."

"Yes, sir. I have found that humans often use small talk during awkward moments. Therefore, I have written a new subroutine for that purpose. How did I do?"

"Perhaps it was a little too non-relevant," Picard replies. "But if you really are interested in small talk, then you should keep your eye on Commander Hutchinson at the reception this afternoon. He's a master!"

Hutchinson is indeed a master, able to ramble endlessly about nothing in particular, and Data engages with him completely, imitating his irrelevance with uncanny vacuity, much to the amusement of Riker and Troi. And yet, the exchanges are endearing; when Hutchinson is senselessly killed moments later, both the crew and the viewer are not just stunned, but saddened.

Small talk might seem awfully innocuous in the context of how to push back against authoritarianism. How could a focus on polite but irrelevant conversation possibly be a tool for resisting autocrats?

At face value, we might see some value in the undeniable positivity of human connection, however inconsequential; and we can grant that even a triviality like small talk can serve as an indicator of societal health.

But what we see in the episode quoted above, "Starship Mine", is that the breezy innocence of Data's chat with Hutchinson has deeper levels; its very shallowness reminds us of the interconnectedness that defines us as a species.

And that interconnectedness makes small talk an important practice, when pushing back against the encroachment of authoritarianism in a society. Historian Timothy Snyder, in his treatise on tyranny, recommends small talk and eye contact as important habits the freedom fighter should employ.

"This is not just polite," he wrote. "It is part of being a citizen and a responsible member of society."

In this we can infer the value he is reminding us to find in our participation in that society. Human contact needs to remain a constant in times of distressing change.

But there's more going on in what Snyder is recommending:

"It is also a way," he continued, "to stay in touch with your surroundings, break down social barriers, and understand whom you should and should not trust."

That's powerful. The idea is, *Know the people around you – for better and worse.*

That's a little discouraging, that it might be as important to use superficial social politeness as a means of scrutinizing our fellow human beings as it is to use it to brighten our days. But the pragmatism of his suggestion is undeniable, as he finally points out,

"If we enter a culture of denunciation, you will want to know the psychological landscape of your daily life."

Sobering. But crucial, all the same.

"We have a deep connection to one another that I've never felt before..."

Cultivate Community

Half a galaxy from home, at the far end of the Beta Quadrant, the *USS Discovery* with Christopher Pike commanding has come across a colony of 21st-century humans from Earth, living simple and technology-free. They were transported to this planet without warning during the Third World War, and have no knowledge of how it was accomplished. Pike and his team note that they have managed some astonishing social innovations, in pursuit of building a permanent and enduring community.[23]

"They awoke here and founded New Eden," an elder informs Pike and his team, once they make contact with the people of the town they explore on the planet's surface.

"But who should they thank for this salvation? Which god?" she continues. "There were so many faiths among them, how could they solve such a quandary?"

Pike and Michael Burnham, having examined the stained

---

[23] In "New Eden", *Star Trek: Discovery* (S2/E2)

glass narratives in the town's church, realize how they did it.

"By combining all religions into one," Pike replies.

Burnham said it another way, during her study of the stained glass windows.

"Anthropologically speaking, it appears they cobbled together a religion based on the primary faiths of Earth."

In the Delta Quadrant, the *USS Voyager* comes across a world settled by ex-Borg – former drones freed from the Collective, living in a community they created themselves after breaking free.[24]

Because the Borg Collective contains captives from hundreds of different races, the freed former drones are likewise a conglomeration of many species. Commander Chakotay explores this with Riley, a member of the community – a human, formerly a Starfleet officer.

"For better or worse, this place has become our home," Riley tells Chakotay. "The people in the cooperative, they're like my ancestors. Texas homesteaders."

"I can understand that, but-"

"We have a deep connection to one another that I've never felt before. Not even with members of my own family. I guess it's because of what we've all gone through together.

"We're creating a society here, one that's based on tolerance, shared responsibility and mutual respect that people like you and I were raised to believe in. We're not about to give it up because it's difficult."

Later, Chakotay meets Orum, another ex-Borg:

"Riley is telling the truth, Commander Chakotay. Look at me. I was Romulan. I was taught to hate humans, the

---

²⁴ In "Unity", *Star Trek: Voyager* (S3/E17)

Federation. But Riley and I are friends now. I'm part of the cooperative."

The authoritarian seeks to divide. By parsing populations into "Loyal" and "Other" and providing each with different rhetoric, he keeps people from seeing for themselves the machinations at work, rearranging their lives to suit his purposes.

Among people living in true community, those kinds of machinations don't remain hidden. When people who live side by side every day reconcile their differing worldviews and refuse to let them distract from their understanding of those they are living alongside, the authoritarian's deceits can't take root.

"We all live in a context, in a society," wrote Richard Haass. "We have a stake in the overall well-being of that society, which in turn translates into our having a stake in the well-being of our fellow citizens. As poet and priest John Donne wrote, 'No man is an island entire of itself; every man is a piece of the continent, a part of the main.' There are both moral and practical reasons for caring about our fellow Americans. The former is simply caring for others for their sake. The question is a familiar one: Am I my brother's or sister's keeper? To some extent we should be and need to be. This teaching can be found in many of the world's major religions. The New Testament instructs, 'Look not every man on his own things, but every man also on the things of others.' In Judaism, the notion is captured by the theme that 'all of Israel are responsible for one another.' Various Hindu texts contain verses that elaborate on the theme of the world as one family, calling on individuals to treat others equally and as they would want to be treated. This sense of obligation to one's fellow man or woman is the basis of a great deal of volunteerism and charity. At best this is an argument for choosing to do good things that assist others; at a minimum, it is an argument for avoiding doing things that injure others.

"There is another reason for caring about others," he

continued. "Doing so reflects our self-interest and is for our own sake. Martin Luther King Jr. made such an argument in his 'Letter from a Birmingham Jail': 'We are caught in an inescapable network of mutuality, tied in a single garment of destiny. Whatever affects one directly affects all indirectly.' In many ways the trajectories of other people's lives intersect with our own and the consequences can be significant and, unfortunately, not always beneficial. Strangers and neighbors alike can be sources of contagion by carrying infectious disease or a burden on public health stemming from abuse of drugs or alcohol. People can turn to crime for a host of reasons and even if there is no intent can act irresponsibly with guns or cars. Then there is the reality that there are those who do not contribute what they could to society and the economy and as a result increase the financial burden of the rest of us. All this adds up to a strong case that the obligation to care for others, be it for their sake or our own, is critical for a democratic society. Teddy Roosevelt, in his inaugural address more than a century ago, posited that 'our relations with the other powers of the world are important, but still more important are our relations among ourselves.'"

Robert Putnam commented on how isolation and loneliness are perilous to democracy, in a *New York Times* interview:

"What we've seen over the last 25 years is a deepening and intensifying of that trend. We've become more socially isolated, and we can see it in every facet in our lives. We can see it in the surgeon general's talk about loneliness. He's been talking recently about the psychological state of being lonely. Social isolation leads to lots of bad things. It's bad for your health, but it's *really* bad for the country, because people who are isolated, and especially young men who are isolated, are vulnerable to the appeals of some false community. I can cite chapter and verse on this: Eager recruits to the Nazi Party in the 1930s were lonely young German men, and it's not an accident that the people who are attracted today to white nationalist groups are lonely young white men. Loneliness: it's bad for your health, but it's also bad for the health of the people around you."

He explores the impact of isolation and loneliness on Americans without community in *Bowling Alone:*

"Without a strong sense of social belonging, individuals are more prone to loneliness and isolation," he wrote. "A sense of belonging is fundamental to human well-being."

And

"In a world of increasing individualism, we must find ways to rebuild the social ties that once held us together."

And

"The more connected we are to our communities, the happier and healthier we tend to be."

And, most tellingly,

"Civic participation is not just a privilege, but a responsibility of every citizen."

And

"People divorced from community, occupation, and association are first and foremost among the supporters of extremism." All the more reason to get to work on cultivating community!

Christopher Pike saw community and mutuality at work in New Eden, as the community's members created their own "single garment of destiny" by prioritizing their mutual support above the form of their genuflections. Faced with forging a new life for themselves beyond the Borg Collective, former Borg from many different races united into one community to form a cooperative, for the purposes of mutual care and support.

In opposing the authoritarian, the cultivation of this sort of community with those unlike ourselves is one of the surest deterrents of the authoritarian's threat.

> *"You may be witnessing the start of a
> new era, not only for Vulcan,
> but for Earth as well."*

Make International Friends

Jonathan Archer, not just the captain of the original *Enterprise* but an architect of the emerging Federation, contributed greatly to that emergence in a series of encounters with other members-to-be of the Federation – Vulcans, Andorians, Tellerites. In particular, an event on Vulcan after a bombing at the United Earth Embassy, in which Archer labors to get to the truth of the bombing, working with a renegade faction of Vulcans ideologues (including a young T'Pau), under the duress of a recalcitrant Starfleet.[25]

The Andorians get into the game when it turns out that another group of Vulcans is developing Xindi-based weapons. Working diligently to get to the truth by bringing humans, Vulcans, and Andorians into cooperation, Archer reveals the truth about the bombing – and clears the way for future

---

[25] In "The Forge", "Awakening", "Kir'Shara", *Star Trek: Enterprise* (S4/E7, 8, 9)

cooperation between the races.

We've already heard from Mark Twain, above, on the power of international experience to diminish our prejudices and open us to diversity. But Timothy Snyder clues us in on another benefit to international friendships: they serve to strengthen us against the authoritarian, by expanding our knowledge base about and resources with which to oppose growing tyranny.

"Learn from peers in other countries," he advised. Our European friends, after all, have a lot more experience with autocrats and tyrants than we do.

It's also advantageous, he points out, to have safe harbors beyond our own borders:

"Keep up your friendships abroad, or make new friends in other countries. The present difficulties in the United States are an element of a larger trend. And no country is going to find a solution by itself. Make sure you and your family have passports.

"The fact that most Americans do not have passports has become a problem for American democracy. Sometimes Americans say that they do not need travel documents, because they prefer to die defending freedom in America. These are fine words, but they miss an important point. The fight will be a long one. Even if it does require sacrifice, it first demands sustained attention to the world around us, so that we know what we are resisting, and how best to do so. So having a passport is not a sign of surrender. On the contrary, it is liberating, since it creates the possibility of new experiences. It allows us to see how other people, sometimes wiser than we, react to similar problems. Since so much of what is happening now is familiar to the rest of the world or from recent history, we must observe and listen."

The rising authoritarianism in the US is being echoed even

now in Europe, and the truth is, we're all in it together – Americans, Hungarians, Ukrainians, Poles. In opposing it, we must be united; like the humans, Vulcans, and Andorians of Jonathan Archer's era, we're simply stronger together.

And we get together by doing just that – getting together.

"I know you're out there. I know you can hear me. Tell me you're on your way. Tell me I'm not going to die alone!"

Let Others Know 'You Are Not Alone'

Aboard Picard's *Enterprise*, Data is in touch with a small child via subspace communication, a little girl on the non-aligned world of Drema IV. That planet has been experiencing geological stresses that endanger the girl and all her people. Because it is not a Federation planet and the inhabitants are unaware of life on other worlds, the Prime Directive applies, and the Enterprise cannot interfere. Data's direct contact with the girl, however, complicates matters.[26]

"Eight weeks ago, I received a transmission, a simple four word message, 'Is anybody out there?'" Data explains to Picard. "I answered it."

"There is a loneliness inherent in that whisper from the

---

[26] In "Pen Pals", *Star Trek: The Next Generation* (S2/E15)

darkness."

"Yes, sir. I am glad that you understand, sir."

"But it didn't end there."

"No, sir. We speak often. It is a young female, humanoid."

"Her society is aware that there is interstellar life?"

"No, sir."

"Oops. Just where does she think you're calling from?"

"I have kept that somewhat vague, sir, but Sarjenka, that is her name, has been quite specific, telling me details of her family and friends. And interspersed among these confidences have been some alarming references."

As the staff is discussing what to do about the situation, the girl calls Data again:

"Data. Data, where are you? Why won't you answer? Are you angry with me? Please, please, I'm so afraid! Data, Data, where are you?"

And with that, Picard decides, "Oh, Data. Your whisper from the dark has now become a plea. We cannot turn our backs."

Answering a Starfleet distress signal, Ben Sisko commands the *Defiant* on a rescue mission to retrieve the sole survivor of the *USS Olympia*:

"...repeat. This is a general distress call. Hello? Is anyone paying attention? I know you're out there. I know you can hear me. So just answer me. Tell me you're on your way! Tell me I'm going to be rescued! Tell me I'm not going to die alone!"[27]

Isolation and loneliness are tough enough to endure in themselves. Human beings are social creatures, through and through; we are not meant to be alone.

But isolation and loneliness are tougher still when accompanied by hopelessness and despair – and that is exactly the burden the authoritarian heaps on those he would put down and repress. The isolation and despair are intended to extinguish hope – and, thereby, opposition.

"In all struggles... strugglers, fighters, resistors or peasant/organic intellectuals have tended to start and sustain the struggles either alone or with very few comrades in arms," wrote Yusuf Serunkuma in *Review of the African Political Economy.* "Because these moments tend to be long and winding, they come with corrosive spells of loneliness - and are often exhausting. The toll could be either mental or material or both."

Serunkuma commented on "a deeply personal, emotional and introspective piece" by alejandra ciriza, in which she "recollects the memories of struggle and exile after the 1976 coup in her home country of Argentina which brought in the murderous government of the *Cono Sur.* ciriza writes that the military junta that headed the coup in 1976 was so brutal that political persecution by the state included, 'systematic use of terror, in broad daylight, forced disappearance, murder, confinement, and censorship, but [also] the methodical inculcation of fear'. Reflecting on this condition, as one of those who had been active in resisting the junta, ciriza recalls the pains of exile, the pain of brutal defeat, and hopelessness about the future: 'It was a harsh isolation. The absences transformed into permanent anguish, the endless searches in

---

[27] In "The Sound of Her Voice", *Star Trek: Deep Space Nine* (S6/E25)

the newspapers looking for a name ... among the fallen'.

"'So, this is what largely defeat is all about,' she writes, capturing the pain of loneliness when friends and comrades have been exiled or murdered. 'The isolation, the rupture of the threads of collective fabric, of the connections with others, so indispensable for us to think and struggle, of loss of emancipatory horizons, which can be envisioned when the masses become conscious of their powers'. These different reflections on loneliness provide a spectrum of reflections covering different modes of struggle."

ciriza was writing in circumstances far harsher than most in the US have ever known, but the dynamic captured is the same: the authoritarian's isolation and disruption do more than sever connection between allies; they generate an immobilizing anguish and pain. It is the duty, then, of those resisting the authoritarian to respond to that.

Data's young friend Sarjenka is lonely and afraid, and is willing to take great risk to maintain connection. Lisa Cusak, marooned after her fellow crewmates have been killed, is losing hope fast. In both cases, Starfleet provided connection and hope.

When we hear a lonely and isolated voice out there on our landscape, losing hope as the clouds gather, we need to answer.

"The challenge is to improve yourself..."

Joining the Quest for Meaning

"The challenge, Mister Offenhouse, is to improve yourself...to enrich yourself. Enjoy it!"
~Picard, to a displaced 20th-century businessman

Near the Romulan Neutral Zone, Picard's *Enterprise* has located an ancient cryogenic spacecraft that originated on Earth centuries earlier. Aboard are three surviving humans from that time, now faced with adapting to life in the 24th century.[28]

"What will happen to us?" asks Ralph Offenhouse, who was a successful businessman in the past. "There's no trace of my money. My office is gone. What will I do? How will I live?"

"This is the twenty-fourth century," Picard replies. "Material needs no longer exist."

"Then what's the challenge?"

---

[28] In "The Neutral Zone", *Star Trek: The Next Generation* (S1/E26)

"The challenge, Mister Offenhouse, is to improve yourself. To enrich yourself. Enjoy it!"

What gives meaning to life?

With the removal of religion from the human equation, the meaning of life can no longer be found in striving for/avoiding imagined eternal rewards or punishments, in the approval of divine beings, or higher purposes defined by holy texts. If life has meaning, it is our responsibility to identify and pursue it within the humanist framework of self-determination and personal industry.

Put another way, humanism does not offer a static, canned definition of the 'meaning of life'. The humanist position – take it or leave it! - is that it is up to each of us as individuals to work out that meaning for ourselves, take it on board, apply it as we will, and never impose what we take to be life's meaning on others, as religion tends to do.

The International Humanist and Ethical Union puts it this way:

"Humanism is a democratic and ethical life stance, which affirms that human beings have the right and responsibility to give meaning and shape to their own lives.

"It stands for the building of a more humane society through an ethic based on human and other natural values in the spirit of reason and free inquiry through human capabilities.

"It is not theistic, and it does not accept supernatural views of reality."

Humanist philosopher Julian Baggini goes several steps more deeply into this question than most, confronting the very phrase "meaning of life", quoted in Copson's *Understanding Humanism*. If the question of humanism offers meaning to life is being asked, he insists that we first ask what "meaning of life" means, and then proceed to see if humanism can muster an answer.

"People are quick to conclude that if there is no creator God, then there is no meaning or purpose to life," he writes. "Yet it is not clear how *with* a creator God there *is* meaning or purpose. For instance, it is often said that we are here to do God's will. If this were true... our lives would have a purpose of the being that created us, but not a purpose for *us*... If we found that our sole purpose was to serve God, then we might think that was a worse fate than to have no predetermined purpose at all. Is it better to be slaves with a role in the universe or to be free people left create a role for ourselves?"

He goes on, "To ask if life has meaning is to ask why it is worth living. And the glib wisecrack that it is better than the alternatives is actually pretty much the whole truth. Alive, we can smell fresh coffee in the morning, see the smile of a person we love, feel our hearts stir to a piece of music, watch the sun rise, laugh at a classic episode of *Father Ted*, and much, much more. If you need to ask why these things are worth doing, you just haven't appreciated what is great about them."

His fellow humanist philosopher A.C. Grayling also challenges the phrase "meaning of life":

"The proper question, in sum, is not 'what is the meaning of life?' but 'What is the meaning that, out of my relationships, my goals, my efforts, my talents, my various doings and interests, my hopes and my desires, I am or should be creating for my life?' Trying to answer it is itself part of life's meaning."

And he continues, "The meaning of your life is the meaning you give it... there is not one thing, a one-size-fits-all thing, that is 'the meaning of life'. People are various, life is various, circumstances differ; there are many ways that life can be good, flourishing and meaningful, just as there are many causes of misery and failure, despair and tragedy. Luck, and things beyond any individual's control, most certainly have their place in determining the character of a life, and all lives encounter difficulties of some kind. But meaning is something that incorporates these things too, and the way they are faced and borne."

The Meaning Frame

In pursuit of a more systematic response, Humanistics University Professor Peter Derkx proposes the concept of a "meaning frame" to capture those components of humanism that fulfill those consequential requirements of a satisfying life, per the descriptions of Baggini and Grayling. This "meaning frame" is itself a variation on the theme of British humanist Harry Stopes-Roe's "life stance", a phrase conveying a structured worldview. "Life stance" has found favor with the International Humanist and Ethical Union, mentioned above; Derkx's version is offered as a means of introducing more flexibility and diversity into the concept.

Derkx begins[12] by quoting Dutch humanist J.P. van Praag and American social psychologist Roy Baumeister, who contend that "the essence of meaning in connection." The latter's book *Meanings of Life* lists four kinds of meaning:
- One experiences one's life as having *purpose*;
- One experiences one's life as having *moral worth*;
- One has *self-worth*;
- One has *competence* or efficacy

Derkx adds three more:
- One's life has *comprehensibility*;
- One's life has *connectedness*;
- One desires *transcendance*

He develops his frame by pointing out that humanism provides *purpose* by actively connecting the activities of the present to positive value in the future; *moral worth* is provided through the humanist project of seeking moral value in one's potential actions and choosing thereby. *Self-worth*, in the humanist frame, is the explicit assignment of positive value to oneself, consciously avoiding comparison to others in the process; and *competence* emerges when the humanist enters into a life shaped by conscious choices and decision, rather than directionlessness and random events.

Comprehensibility, introduced by Derkx's colleague Jan Hein Mooren, refers to the human need for a sense of coherence, cited by Aaron Antonovsky. Humanism's focus on deliberative decision and action, he points out, leans one's life into order and out of chaos, providing that comprehensibility. *Connectedness*, a very general human need, is satisfied in the humanist frame by the active valuing of others as follow-through in seeking out the best in them. As for *transcendence* – defined by Adri Smaling and Hans Alma as "going beyond what is regular, expected, well-known and safe, exploring and reaching for what is new, different, unknown" - is achieved in part for the humanist by the act of moving beyond one's private interests through the embrace of moral values. There is also the human need for wonder and curiosity, per Alma, and Derkx's 'meaning frame' provides it as a by-product of connectedness, which draws the humanist out of the safety and comforts of home into the world, where wonders abound (more on that below).

Thus Derkx's humanist Meaning Frame provides all that religion ever could, in giving the life well-lived substance and value and positive consequence.

Mystery and wonder

Clearing those hurdles, we can affirm that the humanist does indeed have as much access to mystery and wonder as the religious believer. Richard Norman, in his book *On Humanism*, argues that the humanist, via the offerings of scientific exploration, actually enjoys access to even more:

"It is a matter of having an appropriate sense of awe and wonder when confronted with the vastness and complexity of the natural universe," he wrote. "Again a scientific rationalism can promote this rather than dispel it. Humans have, for instance, always felt a sense of awe when contemplating the night sky. How much more so, now that we know more about the vastness of interstellar space and the huge distances from which the light of the stars has traveled?

"Religions, then, have no monopoly on the emotional dimension of the sense of mystery. And its intellectual dimension, the recognition of the limitations of human understanding, is more readily reconcilable with humanist rather than religious thought."

The more we know about the universe, from the standpoint of true knowledge, the bigger and more beautiful it becomes. The embrace of science and reason doesn't blunt our reaction to its beauty; it greatly enhances it.

It seems appropriate that any last word on the mystery and wonder of the natural universe, which certainly inspires and perpetuates our desire to understand our place in it, should be left to the expert – Carl Sagan:

"Life is but a momentary glimpse of the wonder of this astounding universe, and it is sad to see so many dreaming it away on spiritual fantasy."

And this:

"Every aspect of Nature reveals a deep mystery and touches our sense of wonder and awe. Those afraid of the universe as it really is, those who pretend to nonexistent knowledge and envision a Cosmos centered on human beings will prefer the fleeting comforts of superstition. They avoid rather than confront the world. But those with the courage to explore the weave and structure of the Cosmos, even where it differs profoundly from their wishes and prejudices, will penetrate its deepest mysteries."

"You want to talk to me about loyalty? After you broke your oath? Lied to the people of Earth?"

Affirm Truth, Wherever You Find It

On *Deep Space Nine*, Odo receives a message from Weyoun, a Vorta in the service of the Dominion, which is waging a savage war against the Federation. They meet, and Weyoun tells Odo he is defecting – bringing Starfleet the news that the Dominion's Founders (shapeshifters like Odo himself) have hidden motivations: a pandemic has stricken them, and they are dying.[29]

Weyoun has risked everything and turned on the Founders and even his own people in order to bring this news to Odo.

In the end, he sacrifices himself to save Odo's life.

Summoned to Earth by Starfleet Admiral Leyton as a

---

[29] "Treachery, Faith, and the Great River", *Star Trek: Deep Space Nine* (S7/E6)

Dominion invasion seems imminent, Sisko and Odo get on board with gearing up for that invasion, heightening security and taking relatively drastic measures to button up Earth – an initiative that takes Sisko aback with its extremity as he watches troops patrolling the New Orleans streets outside his father's restaurant.[30]

But all is not as it seems, as a Founder Changeling confronts Sisko, mocking him and Starfleet for their paranoia – there are, in fact, only four Changelings on the entire planet, making martial law a ludicrous step. Now suspicious that all is not as it seems, Sisko is determined to get to the truth. And he does, realizing as he gathers the facts that Admiral Leyton is in fact planning a coup d'état. Back on *DS9*, Major Kira provides the smoking gun – evidence that a Starfleet officer on the station has been manipulating the nearby Gamma Quadrant wormhole to create the illusion that the Dominion is preparing to bring an invasion fleet through it.

A showdown follows, and Leyton's conspiracy is exposed.

Seeking out truth, standing on truth, is a cornerstone of resistance of authoritarianism.

"To abandon facts is to abandon freedom," wrote Snyder. "If nothing is true, then no one can criticize power, because there is no basis upon which to do so. If nothing is true, then all is spectacle. The biggest wallet pays for the most blinding lights.

"You submit to tyranny when you renounce the difference between what you want to hear and what is actually the case," he continued. "This renunciation of reality can feel natural and pleasant, but the result is your demise as an individual—and thus the collapse of any political system that depends upon

---

[30] In "Homefront" and "Paradise Lost", *Star Trek: Deep Space Nine*, (S4/E11,12)

individualism."

And it's not just that letting go of fact strengthens tyranny as it weakens liberty; it's that the embrace of truth, across the spectrum of life, fortifies that life.

"Fascists despised the small truths of daily existence, loved slogans that resonated like a new religion, and preferred creative myths to history or journalism," he wrote. "They used new media, which at the time was radio, to create a drumbeat of propaganda that aroused feelings before people had time to ascertain facts. And now, as then, many people confused faith in a hugely flawed leader with the truth about the world we all share. Post-truth is pre-fascism."

Mycielski offers some specifics here, articulating how the authoritarian will make his assault on truth:

- "They will subjugate state media, turning them into a propaganda tube. Then, through convoluted laws and threats they will attempt to control all mainstream media and limit press freedom. They will ban critical press from their briefings, calling them 'liars', 'fake news'. They will brand those media as "unpatriotic", acting against the People. *Fight for every media outlet, every journalist that is being banned, censored, sacked or labelled an "enemy of the state" – there's no hope for freedom where there is no free press.*
- "They will distort the truth, deny facts and blatantly lie. They will try to make you forget what facts are, sedate your need to find the truth. They will feed "post-truths" and "alternative facts", replace knowledge and logic with emotions and fiction. *Always think critically, fact-check and point out the truth, expose ignorance with facts.*
- "They will incite and then leak fake, superficial "scandals". They will smear opposition with trivial accusations, blowing them out of proportion and then

feeding the flame. This is just smokescreen for the legal steps they will be taking towards totalitarianism. *See through superficial topics in mainstream media and focus on what they are actually doing.*"

The phrase "Affirm truth, wherever you find it" is not actually from either Snyder or Mycielski; it's a quote from Rob Bell, an Evangelical pastor – who breaks with his peers in believing that embracing truth is essential for its own sake – even if that truth flies in the face of doctrine and dogma. The message is all the more powerful, given the messenger.

Once you've reached the truth – stand firm on it.

"My gift to you…"

Get in the Habit of Giving

The telepathic Kes is experiencing new abilities that threaten both her life and the integrity of *Voyager*. She is surging with a power she doesn't understand; and, fearing for the safety of her friends, she takes a shuttle and flees the ship.

Once a safe distance from *Voyager*, Kes finds all the energy within her beginning to release.

"My gift to you," are her last words, and as she vanishes, *Voyager* achieves impossible speed. Moments later, they find themselves 9,500 light-years closer to home.[31]

A drifting space probe from a long-dead civilization comes across the path of Picard's *Enterprise*, and it emits a signal that seizes his mind and puts him into an inexplicable coma.[32]

In his mind, Picard is no longer himself, but Kamin, a citizen

---

[31] In "The Gift", *Star Trek: Voyager* (S4/E2)

[32] In "The Inner Light", *Star Trek: The Next Generation* (S5/E25)

of a small town on the planet Kataan. Disoriented, he demands answers of a woman who turns out to be his wife. She doesn't see Jean-Luc Picard; she sees her husband Kamin.

Years pass, in Picard's mind, years in which he lives an increasingly fulfilling life. As his memories of his former existence fade away, he becomes a father, a community leader – and shepherds his friends and family through the tragedy of their world's ending. Kataan's climate is heating beyond the ability of its inhabitants to survive.

Picard awakens on the bridge of the *Enterprise*. Only 20 minutes have passed. The decades he lived in his mind were a journal of sorts, a documentary of the people of Kataan instilled in Picard by the probe – a way for them to be remembered.

And in selecting Picard as the documentarian, they imparted an invaluable gift to a man who has never known the warmth and comfort of family.

"No one has ever become poor by giving," said Anne Frank, and she is in good company. "I have found that among its other benefits, giving liberates the soul of the giver," said Maya Angelou.

And, from Confucius, "He who wishes to secure the good of others has already secured his own."

The act of giving promotes social health in a way that pushes back against those who would corrupt it, according to Timothy Snyder:

"Contribute to good causes," he wrote. "Be active in organizations, political or not, that express your own view of life. Pick a charity or two and set up autopay. Then you will have made a free choice that supports civil society and helps others to do good.

"When Americans think of freedom, we usually imagine a contest between a lone individual and a powerful government.

We tend to conclude that the individual should be empowered and the government kept at bay. This is all well and good. But one element of freedom is the choice of associates, and one defense of freedom is the activity of groups to sustain their members. This is why we should engage in activities that are of interest to us, our friends, our families. These need not be expressly political: Václav Havel, the Czech dissident thinker, gave the example of brewing good beer.

"Insofar as we take pride in these activities, and come to know others who do so as well, we are creating civil society. Sharing in an undertaking teaches us that we can trust people beyond a narrow circle of friends and families, and helps us to recognize authorities from whom we can learn. The capacity for trust and learning can make life seem less chaotic and mysterious, and democratic politics more plausible and attractive."

We can't jump 9,500 light-years, and we can't bestow family on those who have none – but there are more ways to give, and more who need what we can offer, than we can possibly count. It strengthens us, the giver, and it strengthens the receiver – as it weakens the authoritarian.

"I'll fight them every way and any way I can!"

Don't Rule Out Civil Disobedience

At a Federation archaeological site on Camus II, an old flame of Kirk's, Dr. Janice Lester, has discovered ancient alien technology that can take one person's life essence and move it into someone else. Embittered (and more than a little insane) over her perceived ineligibility for Kirk's world of Starfleet captaincy, she subdues him with a phaser stun and switches bodies with him.[33]

As Janice-as-Kirk takes over his role as captain of the *Enterprise* – an erratic display at best – Kirk-as-Janice realizes he is trapped in someone else's body, and that he has been robbed of his identity. No one believes him – until Spock mind-melds with Janice Lester, and realizes he is sensing James Kirk.

Janice-as-Kirk's increasingly authoritarian behavior is already causing great consternation among the senior staff, and responds to Spock's assertions by mocking them, at first – and then more forcefully, when Spock attempts to free

---

[33] In "Turnabout Intruder", *Star Trek: The Original Series* (S3/E24)

"Janice Lester" from the medical confinement Janice-as-Kirk had ordered.

Janice-as-Kirk convenes a court martial, accusing Spock of mutiny, imploring him to give up his claim.

"No, sir. I shall not withdraw a single charge that I have made. You are not Captain Kirk. You have ruthlessly appropriated his body, but the life entity within you is not that of Captain Kirk. You do not belong in charge of the *Enterprise*, and I shall do everything in my power against you."

Janice-as-Kirk flies into a rage, insisting on a vote of the senior officers. Out in the corridor, McCoy and Scotty agree that Spock must be right, and they, too, must stand against the tyrannical imposter. Janice-as-Kirk then declares them guilty of mutiny as well, and orders their executions, over the objections of junior officers Sulu and Chekov.

Soon after, on the bridge, the two discuss what has just happened:

"The captain really must be going mad if he thinks he can get away with an execution," Sulu says.

"Captain Kirk wouldn't order an execution even if he were going mad. That cannot be the captain," Chekov points out.

"What difference does it make who he is? Are we going to allow an execution to take place?"

"If security backs him up, how will we fight him?"

"I'll fight them every way and any way I can," Sulu declares.

Janice-as-Kirk enters the bridge.

"Lieutenant Lysa," he says to the on-duty communications officer, "inform all sectors of my decision. Have each section send a representative to the place of execution on the hangar deck. Mister Chekov, how far to the Benecia Colony?"

"Coming within scanning range," Chekov replies.

"Plot co-ordinates for orbit. Mister Sulu, lock into co-ordinates as soon as orbit is accomplished. Interment will take place on Benecia."

Chekov and Sulu remove their hands from their controls, refusing to follow the orders.

Janice-as-Kirk flies into another rage. "You have received your orders! You will obey my orders! You'll be charged with mutiny!"

They are unmoved, and refuse to comply.

As a fake Jim Kirk imposes a tyrannical authority over the *Enterprise*, its stalwart officers respond with one of the oldest strategies of resistance in history: *civil disobedience.*

It's not really "civil" in this case, since they are officers in a quasi-military order, but the concept is the same – pushing back against an illegitimate authority by refusing to acknowledge it, often at great personal cost.

The Greek playwright Sophocles was a pacesetter in this regard, presenting in *Antigone* a title character who perfectly embodies the concept. Antigone, daughter of Oedipus, defies her father's successor Creon in insisting on a burial for her brother Polynices, declaring that the dictates of her conscience outweigh the king's decree. She ends up paying for her disobedience with her life, a price she declares not too dear.

Henry David Thoreau's treatise on the subject is an American classic:

"I was not made to be forced," he wrote in *On the Duty of Civil Disobedience*. "Let us see who is the strongest."

And this:

"Must the citizen ever for a moment, or in the least degree, resign his conscience to the legislator? Why has every man a conscience, then? I think that we should be men first, and subjects afterward. It is not desirable to cultivate a respect for the law, so much as for the right. The only obligation which I have a right to assume is to do at any time what I think right."

And this:

"A common and natural result of an undue respect of law is, that you may see a file of soldiers, colonel, captain, corporal, privates, powder-monkeys, and all, marching in admirable order over hill and dale to the wars, against their wills, ay, against their common sense and consciences, which makes it very steep marching indeed, and produces a palpitation of the heart."

And this:

""Let your life be a counter-friction to stop the machine. What I have to do is to see, at any rate, that I do not lend myself to the wrong which I condemn."

Civil disobedience can take many forms, of course. The prominent examples in American history include the Boston Tea Party, when New England colonists threw a cargo of British East India Tea into Boston Harbor, flagrantly breaking the law to protest an unjust and exploitative tax; Rosa Parks took her famous bus ride in Montgomery, Alabama, refusing to sit in the back of the bus because her skin color rendered her a second-class citizen in the eyes of her white neighbors. Around the nation, young men burned their draft cards – risking prison – to protest the Vietnam War, which the US government was forcing them to fight for dubious reasons.

An act of law-breaking, an act of rule-breaking; both acts of resistance. And there are still more:

- **Leaking sensitive information.** Leaking information that reveals covert abuses of authority, such as civil rights violations. Also known as "whistleblowing", this form of civil disobedience has often extended to pushback against corporations acting in their own interests at the expense of the public. In cases involving military and other government secrets, it might be considered espionage.

- **Demonstrations.** It is not uncommon, in the US and many other countries, for protesters to stage unregistered marches, rallies, and other demonstrations to protest what they perceive as injustice or abuse of power. This is sometimes problematic, as the stated purpose of such registration is to provide authorities with the opportunity to ensure the safety of the protestors; all too often, in the past, such registration has been withheld, not over safety issues, but to quell protest – which is why many demonstrators will simply employ civil disobedience and protest illegally, rather than be silenced.

- **Sit-ins.** A variation on general demonstrations such as rallies and marches, sit-ins are specifically designed to obstruct traffic or access to buildings or some other inconvenience, as a means of drawing attention to an issue. The idea is to provoke a police response, usually to draw the media, and may include extremes such as handcuffing oneself to a fence or a gate. The actor Martin Sheen, who portrayed a progressive US president on *The West Wing*, prides himself on having been arrested dozens of times at sit-in demonstrations. They are illegal, and therefore attention-getting, for a reason: they carry risk, as such obstruction could potentially create a public hazard by blocking infrastructure in a way that constrains emergency vehicles and personnel.

- **Occupation.** A variation on the sit-in, this form of protest is basically a demonstration that doesn't end: protesters move into an area and just stay there, daring the law to move them. The locale can be a building, a parking lot, a bus station, a public park – any place that people aren't allowed to stay indefinitely. This, too, can result in breaking the law. The Occupy Wall Street movement, a 2011 populist movement in which tens of thousands of New York City citizens protested the 2008 bank bailouts and the 2010 US Supreme Court Citizens United ruling, was such an occupation. It lasted 59 days.

Thoreau was, of course, exactly right: failure to stand up to authoritarian abuses and moral offenses is, in its own way, likewise a moral offense; no one stands innocent when they ignore their own impulses of conscience.

Is this risky behavior? Of course it is, as the fictional Antigone discovered. Not everyone becomes a hero for doing the right thing, as Rosa Parks did.

Chekov and Sulu – and, of course, Spock – got it right. They stood up against a tyrant even when they realized it might cost them their lives. That's a moment we hope will never come; but if it ever does, what will you do?

"These words must apply to everyone, or they mean nothing!"

Defending Our Institutions

Captain Kirk and his crew are at Omega IV, encountering the *USS Exeter*, commanded by Kirk's peer Ronald Tracy. Beaming aboard the unresponsive Exeter, they find that its crew has been killed by a strange disease – contracted on the planet below.[34]

Beaming down, they find that Tracy has ingratiated himself with one of two major ethnic groups, the Kohms, going so far as to violate the Prime Directive by equipping them with phasers, which they use against their enemies, the Yangs.

The Yangs and the Kohms are somewhat ridiculous stand-ins for Earth's Yankees and Communists, making the story a Cold War parable about the struggle between democracy and communism. Even so, as Kirk learns that the Yangs have a Constitution that is eerily American and proceeds to bring forth a speech about it, an important point about the struggle

---

[34] In "The Omega Glory", *Star Trek: The Original Series* (S2E23)

between democracy and communism emerges:

"Hear me! Hear this! Among my people, we carry many such words as this from many lands, many worlds. Many are equally good and are as well respected, but wherever we have gone, no words have said this thing of importance in quite this way.

"Look at these three words written larger than the rest, with a special pride never written before or since," Kirk pontificates to his Yang captors. "Tall words proudly saying *We the People!* That which you call *Ee'd Plebnista* was not written for the chiefs or the kings or the warriors or the rich and powerful, but for *all* the people! Down the centuries, you have slurred the meaning of the words, 'We, the people of the United States, in order to form a more perfect union, establish justice, ensure domestic tranquility, provide for the common defense, promote the general welfare, and secure the blessings of liberty to ourselves and our posterity, do ordain and establish this Constitution!' These words and the words that follow were not written only for the Yangs, but for the Kohms as well! They must apply to everyone, or they mean nothing! Do you understand?"

As silly as the episode itself is, the importance of what Kirk is doing can scarcely be understated. He is defending, not just the content of the Constitution, but the institution it defines. He is underscoring for the Yangs that they are a people – not just their nation, but a *planetary* people – and that the institution they seek to perpetuate is of ultimate importance.

Again, Tim Snyder makes the point:

"It is institutions that help us to preserve decency," he wrote. "They need our help as well. Do not speak of 'our institutions' unless you make them yours by acting on their behalf."

Kirk's denunciation of autocracy, the 'chiefs and kings and the rich and powerful', is a crucial exemplar of this principle. He is imploring Cloud William and the other Yangs to make the Constitution their own, to display the ownership and investment that Snyder is portraying as essential to any society worth fighting for.

"Institutions do not protect themselves," Snyder added, "so choose an institution you care about and take its side."

It's important to note, in considering *Trek*'s take on Snyder's idea, that the institution being defended may constitute a "side" – but that the principles it encapsulates is not a matter of sides. Yes, democracy must push back against autocracy – but the war of ideas is ultimately just that, a struggle between two concepts of human governance. That's not the same as war between people, who need not make war on one another just because they disagree. Kirk makes the point near the end of his speech: "These words and the words that follow were not written only for the Yangs, but for the Kohms as well! They must apply to everyone, or they mean nothing!

On the one hand, we might be tempted to cynically observe that Kirk's line has a Cold War-era saving-the-world-for-democracy feel; but on the other, it can be more encouragingly (and appropriately) read as Kirk's embrace of *Trek*'s universal equality theme.

"You have to take chances, stand out in a crowd!"

Get in the Game

Q is screwing with Captain Picard again, intervening in the moment of his death to pose as the Almighty. But it takes a useful and instructive turn as Picard processes his regret over the recklessness of his youth. Q decides to teach Picard a lesson by allowing him to relive that youth, it's-a-wonderful-life-style, and a more thoughtful and prudent Cadet Jean-Luc Picard avoids the confrontation that resulted in his artificial heart.[35]

But upon returning to the present in this now-modified timeline, he finds that he is still fated to serve on the *Enterprise* – but as a lowly analyst of no real merit or accomplishment. He approaches Riker and Troi in Ten Forward:

"Please," he tells them, "This is important to me. I believe that I can do more."

"Hasn't that been the problem all along?" Troi replies. "Throughout your career you've had lofty goals, but you've

---

[35] In "Tapestry", *Star Trek: The Next Generation* (S6/E15)

never been willing to do what's necessary to attain them."

"Would that be your evaluation as well, Commander?"

"I think I have to agree with the Counsellor," Riker answers. "If you want to get ahead, you have to take chances, stand out in a crowd, get noticed."

Stand out. Take chances. That's Riker's formula for getting things done. It's not enough to be competent; we have to be proactive, perhaps even aggressive.

"Someone has to," wrote Timothy Snyder. "It is easy to follow along. It can feel strange to do or say something different. But without that unease, there is no freedom. Remember Rosa Parks. The moment you set an example, the spell of the status quo is broken, and others will follow."

Richard Haass added this:

"A democracy depends on the participation of its citizens," he wrote. It is rule by the people rather than of the people. Yes, in a representative democracy elected and appointed officials wield a great deal of power, but the point is that this power is derived from those who elect them and give them the power to act. The Declaration of Independence explicitly makes this point: 'Governments are instituted among men, deriving their just powers from the consent of the governed.' This all requires, though, that citizens take an active part in their democracy. It may seem hard to believe that they would not, in that people fought and died for the American colonies to become an independent, democratic country not subjugated to a king or to a parliament they had no influence over. But in fact many Americans do not participate actively in their democracy. It is ironic that we have gone to war for the right of others to be free but all too often seem content not to take advantage of the reality that we are."

He provided some concrete examples (also invoking Rosa Parks):

"There are many other ways to bolster democracy beyond

voting and direct involvement in politics. What is more, you need not be famous or powerful to make a difference. As former Secretary of Defense James Mattis pointed out, 'The impact of participation trickles up. Rosa Parks didn't start out by taking on all of Jim Crow; she started out by taking a seat on a local bus.' A group of parents initiated what turned out to be a successful recall of three members of San Francisco's school board in 2022. One woman, after losing a family member in an automobile accident, came up with the idea that became Mothers Against Drunk Driving (MADD), an organization that over the past four decades has saved countless lives. Or take gerrymandering, the process by which the majority party in a state legislature draws the lines of congressional or state legislative districts in an attempt to disadvantage the minority party. (A second consequence of gerrymandering is to increase extremism, as districts tend to be dominated by one or the other party, thereby reducing the need for candidates to attract votes from the political center in order to build a majority.) In Michigan, the entire process was turned around by a woman with no political experience who in the wake of the 2016 election used social media to launch a volunteer movement that took the power to draw districts from the state government and awarded it to an independent commission."

And this, from Robert Putnam:

"A successful democracy requires active participation and engagement from its citizens."

Troi and Riker are right: 'lofty goals' are meaningless without the will and determination to pursue them; you have to take chances, stand out in the crowd.

"Never give up! Never surrender!"

Galaxy Quest Joins the Mission

We'll give the last word on Away Team action to *Galaxy Quest*, *Trek*'s beloved stepchild – a tale built around the adventures of the *NSEA Protector*, an almost-*Enterprise* manned by a crew that lovingly parodies our Starfleet idols.

Captain Peter Quincy Taggart, who commands the *Protector*, mimics the bumper-sticker pearls that permeate *Trek* lore – "Fascinating," "He's dead, Jim," "I'm a doctor, not a," "Engage!", and so on – with one of his own, which we see in an episode clip displayed at a fan convention:

"Never give up! Never surrender!"

Exactly right.

Perseverance is the most important factor in resisting the authoritarian. All the others come to nothing if they are, in the end, abandoned.

Mycielski's essay provides a list of rules centered on perseverance:

- **Don't stay indifferent.** "It will concern you eventually. It *will* concern your family, your friends.

Voice your objection *immediately!* Resist!"

- **Expose them.** "They thrive on *fear & ignorance.* Expose their scaremongering, show flaws in their arguments. They will try to distort *facts*, rewrite history – *educate* people around you."
- **Organize, mobilize!** "They're well-organized, so should you be. *Flood the streets.* They *will* back off when they see your numbers."
- **Don't let them divide you.** "... into different classes of citizens, 'true Americans', 'patriots' vs. 'traitors', 'enemies of the state'. You're *all* citizens, *one* nation – make diversity your *strength!*"
- **Don't give up.** "Don't get tired, and don't try to wait it out. Don't hope it will pass. It *won't.*"
- **Once they're out, keep them out.** "If you don't get them to back off or to step down, you better make goddamn *sure* that when the next elections come, assuming there's still any democracy left, *no one* will vote for the same bastards again!"

That level of commitment is not just essential – it's existential. If enough people don't reach it, and stick with it, democracy is over.

And achieving that commitment requires a solid foundation of values that inspire and support it. They are values *Trek* modeled for us, again and again, and they are presented in the pages that follow.

PRIME DIRECTIVES

Trek's Call to Commitment

Commitment to Core Values

Before we can answer a call to action, we have to do a self-assessment; it's not enough to simply stand against something; we must be clear on what it is we're *for*. What we're fighting against is blatantly clear; what we're fighting *for* is not always so easily articulated.

The answer, of course, is that we're fighting for our values; we're fighting for the things we believe in. It's important, then, to define those things as precisely as we can, and to be able to articulate them to others.

In the *Trek* universe, those values and principles are clear: they include an opposition to tyranny, of course, but its reciprocal – egalitarianism – is embraced. Diversity and social equality are paramount; truth, the greater good, the rights of all, freedom for everyone – these all naturally follow. Ensuring that everyone has a voice, and deriving an enduring unity from acceptance of that idea, wraps it all together.

A renewed commitment to those values, expressed below in *Trek* terms, is the starting point of meaningful action in resisting the authoritarian.

"With the first link, the chain is forged. The first speech censored, the first thought forbidden, the first freedom denied, chains us all irrevocably."

Resisting Authoritarianism

"The revolution is successful. But survival depends upon drastic measures. Your continued existence represents a threat to the well-being of society. Your lives mean slow death to the more valued members of the colony. Therefore, I have no alternative but to sentence you to death. Your execution is so ordered.."

~Kodos, Governor of Tarsus IV

In 2246, Kodos - the governor of the Tarsus IV colony - is faced with the starvation of the 8,000 Federation colonists under his governance when a fungus destroys the food supply. In a terrifying totalitarian gesture, he orders half the colonists killed so that the remainder might survive on what little food remained until relief arrives. He himself decides who would live and who would die.[36]

When a Klingon exchange officer aboard Picard's *Enterprise* is revealed to be a Romulan collaborator, retired Admiral Norah Satie boards the ship to conduct an investigation. In the process, she uncovers a low-level member of Dr. Crusher's staff who had a Romulan grandfather and lied to Starfleet about it. Satie's investigation becomes increasingly paranoid, rife with accusation, until she casts suspicion upon Picard himself, citing his subjugation by the Borg. When Picard takes the stand in his own defense and quotes Satie's own father, citing his rejection of authoritarian disregard for rights and freedoms, Satie becomes enraged, and her witch hunt is shut down by the head of Starfleet Security.[37]

What the media calls "the War on Woke" is essentially an Authoritarian war on non-Authoritarian values. Conversely, the values embraced by those considered "Woke" are egalitarian – anti-authoritarian – values. This isn't the only framing we can apply to the Woke conflict, but it's by far the most substantial.

Authoritarianism, then, is an essential issue to be considered when viewing "Woke" thought through the *Star*

---

[36] In "The Conscience of the King", *Star Trek: The Original Series* (S1/E13)

[37] In "The Drumhead", *Star Trek: The Next Generation* (S4/E21)

Trek lens.

Alpha males

In most primate cultures, the alpha male rules.

A single individual, more powerful than his peers, governs the group by means of strength and intimidation, and in the process inculcates fear in others, takes females at will, and enjoys the highest level of privilege – until toppled from power by a superior challenger. So the story goes, among apes and throughout human history.

The assumption is that we naturally conform to this 'alpha' framework of authority.

But if we are more bonobo than chimpanzee, it no longer makes sense; and if we truly are off course, socially – having screwed up millennia of cooperative social order when we ceased to be migratory – then the idea of alpha humans no longer makes sense.

This is what we're talking about when we invoke the term *authoritarianism*. It is used in both political science (to describe the political orientation of a nation-state) and psychology (to describe the dynamics of leader-and-follower, where authoritarianism is the rule). It does not differ significantly, in social terms, from what we observe in chimpanzees.

And when it took hold of humankind, it took hold big: for many thousands of years, our sociopolitical systems have been far more authoritarian than not.

Authoritarianism strips the individual of self-determination. By centralizing authority in an individual, it strips the group of the benefit of pooled knowledge and decision-making skills. By awarding group rule according to personal power, rather than according to actual leadership merits, it represents a danger to the group that amplifies over time.

The authoritarian regimes that have come and gone over

the millennia that human beings have been civilized are countless. Even in the modern era, the age of democracy, authoritarianism continues to rise up, threatening to return us to a sociopolitically captive state.

This couldn't have happened in the Paleolithic. Human survival hinged on multiple axes, not just one: the group required the leadership of a long-term planner, able to anticipate environmental conditions and food supplies months in advance; adept pattern-finders were needed, individuals able to sense weather change and changes in the behavior of prey; and fast-response captains were needed, in moments of sudden attack from predators.

That's not a single leader – that's several, each with a different skill set...a different cognitive style.

Among chimpanzees, authoritarian leadership limits the tribe; it is not able to organize beyond swarming on prey and internal power struggle. It is a constant competition for the top spot, with no attention to the social development of the tribe.

Among the bonobos, leadership is distributed, as it is in democracies. No one individual member of the tribe holds absolute power, and anyone who tries is rapidly slapped down.

Put simply: when we enabled authoritarianism, we were stepping backward, not forward – and we created a danger that threatens us today, possibly more than it ever has before.

What the expert says

The pacesetter in the academic study of authoritarianism is Bob Altemeyer, retired professor of psychology at the University of Manitoba. The most aggressive investigator of authoritarianism for more than three decades, Altemeyer's books on the subject are essential reading for any who would undertake its study.

Long established in academic circles, Altemeyer came to national attention when his explanation of authoritarian behaviors in American politics made their way into the polemics of John Dean (of Watergate fame). At Dean's urging, Altemeyer wrote a book on the subject for laypeople.[1]

Altemeyer has, not surprisingly, had a great deal to say about Donald Trump.

"Authoritarian followers in America today are tremendously energized by fear and anger," he wrote in March 2016. "They're scared, and they want someone really strong and confident to protect them. It's a very natural, understandable reaction.

"Wanna-be tyrants in a democracy are just comical figures on soapboxes when they have no following. So the real threat lay coiled in parts of the population itself, it was thought, ready someday to catapult the next Hitler to power with their votes."

His explanation of the thinking of authoritarian followers illuminates their choice of Donald Trump:

"Research suggests that 20-25% of the adults in North America are highly vulnerable to a demagogue who would incite hatred of various minorities to gain power. These people are waiting for a tough "man on horseback" who will supposedly solve all our problems through the ruthless application of force. When such a man gains prominence, you can expect the authoritarian followers to mate devotedly with the authoritarian leader, because each gives the other something they desperately want: the feeling of safety for the followers, and the tremendous power of the modern state for the leader.

Not all Trump voters qualify as authoritarian followers, Altemeyer wrote, "but they likely compose his hard-core base. Furthermore, many authoritarian followers [supported] Senator Ted Cruz for religious reasons." He went on to predict "most of them [will] slide into the Trump ranks once Cruz drops out of the race. By summer [2016], the vast majority of authoritarian followers in the United States will likely be for Trump."

Which, of course, is exactly what happened.

As for what happens next, "If you believe that a President

Trump would be a very stiff test of democracy in the United States, then what can you do?... Well, it's not going to be easy changing highly aggressive, dogmatic, insular people who will dismiss you out of hand as the enemy... they have been that way for most of their lives, and they have built a lot of supports, including straight-out denial, to keep their views intact.

"One suspects they will feel even more betrayed if... [Trump] turns out to have been conning them all along, too. But he is going to keep telling them he's one of them, and keep them scared and angry while selling himself as the Toughest Guy They Ever Met. Authoritarian followers are always waiting for The Leader, and now they firmly believe they've found him."

Here's a list of traits Altemeyer observes in authoritarian followers:

1. They are highly ethnocentric, highly inclined to see the world as their in-group versus everyone else. Because they are so committed to their in-group, they are very zealous in its cause.
2. They are highly fearful of a dangerous world. Their parents taught them, more than parents usually do, that the world is dangerous. They may also be genetically predisposed to experiencing stronger fear than most people do.
3. They are highly self-righteous. They believe they are the "good people" and this unlocks a lot of hostile impulses against those they consider bad.
4. They are aggressive. Given the chance to attack someone with the approval of an authority, they will lower the boom.
5. They are highly prejudiced against racial and ethnic minorities, non-heterosexuals, and women in general.
6. Their beliefs are a mass of contradictions. They have highly compartmentalized minds, in which opposite beliefs exist side-by-side in adjacent

boxes. As a result, their thinking is full of double standards.

7. They reason poorly. If they like the conclusion of an argument, they don't pay much attention to whether the evidence is valid or the argument is consistent.

8. They are highly dogmatic. Because they have gotten their beliefs mainly from the authorities in their lives, rather than think things out for themselves, they have no real defense when facts or events indicate they are wrong. So they just dig in their heels and refuse to change.

9. They are very dependent on social reinforcement of their beliefs. They think they are right because almost everyone they know, almost every news broadcast they see, almost every radio commentator
they listen to, tells them they are. That is, they screen out the sources that will suggest that they are wrong.

10. Because they severely limit their exposure to different people and ideas, they vastly overestimate the extent to which other people agree with them.

11. And thinking they are "the moral majority" supports their attacks on the "evil minorities" they see in the country.

12. They are easily duped by manipulators who pretend to espouse their causes when all the con artists really want is personal gain.

13. They are largely blind to themselves. They have little self-understanding and insight into why they

think and do what they do.

Altemeyer's Global Change Game

Altemeyer writes of some experiments he conducted with a team in 1994. They involved the Global Change Game, a simulation of international-level interactions between groups of students, meant to explore issues affecting the planet and humankind as a whole.

The game is played on a map the size of a basketball court. A group of 70 students or so play the game together, each assigned to one of 10 regions of the world, representing 100 million people. Assets are distributed among the regions, and each has its own set of issues to deal with: health, hunger, deforestation, climate change, energy shortages, encroaching desert, economic instability, international trade, inequality – all of these and more can appear on the horizon of any world region.

Three of the regions are nuclear superpowers. Conventional military power is distributed as it is in the real world, and several start off the game with indigenous poverty – again, as in
the real world. Facilitators (faculty members) present each region with problems, and it is left to the teams in each region to reach out to request or offer aid, to enter into alliances, to band together to solve problems or oppose one another and create new ones.

Several of the students declare themselves "Elites" – leaders – and the game allows for such players to squirrel away some of their region's wealth for themselves.

Regions can enter into trade agreements, take in refugees, pollute the oceans, offer humanitarian aid, screw up the world economy, and even declare nuclear war (which ends the game by default). After 40 simulated years of international activity, the game is declared over, and points are tallied to determine the winning region.

The Low-Authoritarians. Altemeyer's innovation was to populate one night's run of the game purely with students who had scored low on his RWA scale – students low in Authoritarianism (the students were not made aware that their RWA scores had anything to do with the game). These students managed to achieve world peace and international cooperation. The 10 Elites (seven men, three women) joined together on Tasmania whenever a crisis arose and solved the problem together.

The three nuclear superpowers chose to disarm, and no war broke out during the playing of the game. An ozone depletion crisis announced by the facilitators was solved with the combined economic support of the wealthiest nations and advanced technology. There were several hundred million deaths resulting from disease and starvation in poverty-stricken countries (Europe sent aid – North America refused). World population at the end of the game was 8.7 billion, but resources
were distributed worldwide in such a way as to support almost all of them. Overall, Altemeyer considered it a great success.

The High-Authoritarians. The following night, the game was repeated – this time with students who had all scored high on the Authoritarian scale. The Elites (all male) declined to disarm, and instead began heavy militarization. The Middle East region immediately doubled oil prices. The Soviet Union prepared to invade North America. A nuclear exchange followed soon after, ending the game.

The facilitators turned off the lights and described the effects of nuclear winter to the students before restarting the game. This time, the Soviet Union invaded China, killing 400 million. The Elite from the Middle East called a United Nations meeting, but nothing came of it.

The ozone depletion crisis occurred, but no cooperative

activity was attempted. The European region made some independent efforts to reduce emissions, but the problem got steadily worse. Poverty and population growth went unchecked around the world. Rather than address their nation's economic challenges, the Elites maneuvered for personal power. Alliances were formed, with stronger partners forcing weaker ones to buy in.

At the end of 40 simulated years, the planet was coming apart, facing mounting crises, armed to the teeth and ready for holocaust. A total of 1,700 million people were dead. The Elites had plundered their regions for personal wealth.

And these were college students!

"There they were, in a big room full of people *just like themselves*, and they all turned their backs on each other and paid attention only to their own group," Altemeyer wrote later. "They too were all reading from the same page, but write large on their page was, 'Care About Your Own; We Are NOT All In This Together'."

The implications of these experiments are staggering. These two groups of students varied *only* in their test scores on the Right-Wing Authoritarian Scale; in every other way, they were typical college students, ages 18-22, predominantly white, middle-class, with age-appropriate concerns.

Yet when faced with the opportunity to cooperate or enter into conflict, their differing levels of Authoritarianism caused them to behave entirely differently.

Think about that for a moment. If that can happen in two evenings of game play among young people, it is no surprise to see what we see in the world around us today and throughout history, when power is placed in the hands of adults with these same tendencies and impulses.

Altemeyer and the authoritarian mind

Most of the contents of the Authoritarian mind have come under Altemeyer's scrutiny. In his dozens of studies over the years, he has made use of many instruments, measuring everything from ethnocentricity to dogmatism to logical fallacy. The collective result is a remarkably sharp image of that mind, one that will be familiar to anyone who has that belligerent Fox News-watching uncle who can't shut up about what he heard yesterday on talk radio.

Altemeyer isn't the only one. A number of social scientists have conducted studies investigating the personality features that seem to define Authoritarians. They collectively form a cognitive portrait that is both familiar and remarkably consistent.

Prejudice and bigotry

Altemeyer developed an instrument for measuring an individual's level of ethnocentrism, the Manitoba Ethnocentrism Scale. Subjects rate the truth or falsehood of statements about members of other ethnicities on a scale of -4 to +4, yielding an index of ethnocentric orientation that can be correlated with results on other instruments, such as his RWA scale. In repeated experiments in both Canada and the United States, subjects who scored high on one strongly tended to score high on the other.

He noted that Authoritarian followers who were prejudiced against one ethnic group tended to be prejudiced toward them all – and toward other out-groups, such as homosexuals, as well (this finding has long been established by social psychologists). "Authoritarian followers dislike so many kinds of people, I have called them 'equal opportunity bigots'."

As mentioned in the chapter "A Sociopolitical Family Portrait", Authoritarians are often religious fundamentalists. It's an identity marker, Altemeyer noted, and that reinforced the Authoritarian Us, as noted in the chapter "Authoritarian 'Us' v. Egalitarian 'Them'". He put all of this together in yet another instrument, the Religious Ethnocentrism Scale.

The scale measures the degree to which the subject feels their religion should be the national religion; the degree to which other religions should be ignored; the undesirability of mixing with those with differing beliefs, and so on. For good measure, is also measures the subject's level of disagreement with statements stressing the equality of different religions and the worthiness of religious Others. Unsurprisingly, high-RWAs who identified as fundamentalist Christians scored high in religious ethnocentrism.

Then Altemeyer went a step further, wondering if those who did score high on the Ethnocentrism scale were open to this truth about themselves. He added a question to the test, asking the subject if they would wish to know their score if it turned out it showed them to be highly prejudiced?

In one such experiment, 76% of the low-RWA subjects said they would want to know their score; only 55% of the high-RWAs wanted to know. Then, for clarification, he reversed the question, in a subsequent experiment: the final question asked if the subject if they would wish to know their score if it awarded them a *low* score? The low-RWA subjects scored about the same – 71%; but this time, 77% of the high-RWAs wanted to know their score. Conclusion: low-RWAs are equally interested in good or bad news about themselves, while high-RWAs are very open to good news but less open to bad.

Altemeyer's curiosity was derived from noting that highly prejudiced people tend to deny being so. This lack of self-awareness, he concluded, was essentially tribal: "If you spend a lot of time around rather prejudiced people," he wrote, "you can easily think your own prejudices are normal."

Why some people love authoritarians

I've written in the past that authoritarianism is not necessarily a good thing or a bad thing in and of itself, but becomes constructive or destructive depending on the social context in which it presents.

I hope I've gotten better at writing about the subject and conveying the key ideas, because we're living in an increasingly-authoritarian world, and that's not a good thing, and it's important to talk about it openly and frequently. To that end, I've discovered a short video of exceptional clarity that explains the subject concisely, yet insightfully. The YouTube link to the video is given below.

I want to summarize its contents, but before I do that, I'll briefly recap the pros and cons of Authoritarianism and its opposite, Egalitarianism.

Authoritarian personalities tend to:

- Desire strong leadership
- Obey authority
- Favor hierarchical social order
- Abhor uncertainty
- Resist change
- Feel unsafe, in a wide range of circumstances
- Believe in zero-sum scenarios
- Be very loyal
- Contribute generously to the well-being of the tribe

For context, let's remember that egalitarian personalities tend to:

- Prefer decision-by-consensus to the leadership of

an individual
- Embrace change
- Seek novelty
- Take risks
- Distrust authority
- Be more loyal to ideas than to people
- Be more comfortable with uncertainty
- Favor an equal, distributed social order
- Contribute generously to the well-being of the tribe)

Taken as a whole, it's easy to see that all of these traits potentially have considerable merit in a community; there is room for all of them, and a role for every member, whichever traits they possess.

In Paleolithic societies, individuals with the Authoritarian traits listed above (remember, these are ultimately genetic personality and behavioral factors, not political or ideological distinctions) would have made a good Fire-Tender – a person who could be counted on to safeguard the tribe through the long night by keeping the bonfire going, to discourage attacks by predators.

But we are not living in the Paleolithic Era anymore. And the *mis*-application of Authoritarian tendencies, given our utterly different modern context, can be catastrophic. A modern Authoritarian may tend to:
- Submit to an unworthy leader simply because they make them feel safe;
- Be vulnerable to manipulation by way of falsehoods triggering fear responses;
- Accept misinformation about those in other tribes designed to render them "dangerous" or "enemies";
- Believe in zero-sum scenarios (where there must be a loser for every winner) without justification,

creating a false defensiveness;
- Be dismissive of facts, data, reason, logic, and evidence, when they challenge ideas or beliefs that promote an emotional feeling of safety and security;
- Be willing to suspend equality and fairness, and become accepting of unethical behavior in a leader, if feelings of dread or danger are present.

And this describes what we see all around us, of course, most every day today. Authoritarianism is commonplace; its disciples are numerous. And there is no shortage of social dominators waiting to exploit them.

Now, to the video. It can be found here, if you wish to check it out yourself:

https://www.youtube.com/watch?v=qw8yJ92c_Ds

It opens with the citing of a 2017 National Academy of Sciences study, "Dominant Leader vs. Prestige Leader", which found that people living in zip codes with a history of economic hardship were more likely to support authoritarian leaders in their communities.

It then cites another 2017 study from CNBC, "Why Voters Might Be Choosing Authoritarian Leaders", a three-decade inquiry that surveyed people all over the world, finding that people tend to lean toward Authoritarian leaders in times of economic uncertainty – and that in such times, they are more likely to accept the suspending of democratic norms and to be more tolerant of unethical behavior in their leaders.

It notes a study on Pacific Standard, "The Terrifying Trait That Trump Triggers", which quantifies Authoritarians of making up roughly one-third of the populations of 29 different democracies around the world, but that in such countries, the tendencies of these Authoritarians tend to remain dormant until triggered by some threat (real or perceived). This brings us to the conclusion that it is not that economic uncertainty or other social threats cause people to become Authoritarian, but that 1/3 of the population already possesses Authoritarian tendencies, and threats will cause those tendencies to emerge.

The video explains that the Authoritarian mindset is all-pervasive, not just a batch of situational responses. Authoritarians, for instance, prioritize certain qualities in their children over others – obedience, good manners, and good behavior over independence, curiosity, and critical thinking.

Finally, the video noted that a 2017 *Politico Magazine* study, "Predicting Whether You're a Trump Supporter", reported that an Authoritarian mindset was the sole statistically significant variable predictive of Trump support.

In our current national moment, we see that Authoritarians seem impervious to all inputs from anyone *but* the strongman leaders they follow: no amount of new information, data, facts, logic, or reason can penetrate their thinking. And this should be no surprise; they consider all such inputs to be suspect, efforts to subvert them, dangers to be resisted at all costs. Their emotional investment in the sense of safety and security they derive from their tribe supersedes everything else.

But we need people of *all* cognitive styles and mindsets in the world today, despite the dangers of those misapplied. Everyone has value, and everyone can contribute meaningfully. But an explicitly Authoritarian society under an explicitly Authoritarian strongman leader is the path to ruin: it will result in the loss of liberty, the proliferation of inequality, a landscape of manipulation and persecution. Authoritarianism must be kept in check.

The solution, per the video, is to support and promote those social policies that promote safety and stability, which reduce the triggering of Authoritarian responses – fair taxation, readily-available healthcare, affordable education, sustainable energy, free and fair elections. The presence of such resources promote feelings of safety and security, diminishing the threat posed by social dominators hoping to acquire power.

Rising Authoritarianism today

Authoritarianism is rising in the US today – and around the world. The intense interconnectedness of everything and everyone, enabled by the Internet and the social media it hosts, makes the work of authoritarian leaders easier than it's ever been, and empowers those leaders to spray the disinformation, propaganda, and toxic rhetoric all over their followers like a firehose.

Even experts like Altemeyer are hard-pressed to produce a solution to this problem, though one ray of hope is that the mindset is largely biological; authoritarianism is enabled in individual minds by a propensity for greater fear than most, combined with a lower level of social information processing. Those are genetically-linked brain features, making it probable that there's a limit to the number of authoritarian-leaning minds in any given population. Statistics from around the world suggest that that number is roughly 35 percent.

It should also be clear to even the most casual observer of today's flame wars on social media that there is no talking an authoritarian follower off the ledge. It is useless to argue with them, for all the reasons Altemeyer (and others) have articulated.

What's the Woke *Trek* response here? A big part of it is the pursuit of cognitive diversity, already covered above; in a nutshell, the biggest step forward is to *break up or dilute social echo chambers everywhere you can.* Authoritarianism is weakened when diversity is strengthened.

Oh, and *vote...*

"The first duty of every Starfleet officer is to the truth!"

Integrity in the Public Square

Young Wesley Crusher has done a bad, bad thing. A cadet at Starfleet Academy, he is part of the elite Nova Squadron, a flight team akin to an interplanetary version of the Blue Angels. In a terrible accident, one of the team has just died; at the urging of squadron leader Nick Locarno, the team was practicing a forbidden maneuver, the Kolvoord Starburst, and things went south.[38]

An official inquiry into the incident has begun, and the surviving team members – Wesley included – are obfuscating, to hide the fact that their teammate died because they were attempting something so egregiously dangerous. But Geordi La Forge and Captain Picard figure out what really happened, and Picard realizes that Wesley has testified falsely under oath. He confronts Wesley in his ready room:

"The first duty of every Starfleet officer is to the truth, whether it's scientific truth, or historical truth, or personal truth!" Picard firmly insists. "It is the guiding principle upon which Starfleet is based! If you can't find it within yourself to

---

[38] In "The First Duty", *Star Trek: The Next Generation* (S5/E19)

stand up and tell the truth about what happened, you don't deserve to wear that uniform!"

Picard's angry rebuke of Wesley may seem a little over-the-top, but it's very much in keeping with the ethos he and his officers exude. They are scrupulously honest individuals; it would never occur to them to behave dishonestly. They count on that integrity in one another, and offer it to those they encounter as a benefit of the doubt.

Not all Starfleet officers come by this integrity so easily. Our beloved Captain Kirk could lie with the best of them. Recall the time when he and Spock, misplaced in 1930 New York City, are caught intruding in the cellar of Edith Keeler's mission, and he blames it on the cold.

"A lie is a poor way to say hello," she chastises. Guess he's not so good at it.[39]

He and Spock both do better when, dispatched (presumably) by Section 31, they invade Romulan territory to steal a cloaking device. It's on this occasion that we first hear the legend, later adopted (even by Spock) as fact, that 'Vulcans cannot lie'. They both pretend that the incursion was actually a burst of power mania from an unhinged Kirk – but, of course, they are acting on Starfleet's behalf, and they are indulging in spycraft.[40]

Under arrest and making an official statement, Spock says, "I say now and for the record that Captain Kirk ordered the *Enterprise* across the Neutral Zone on his own initiative and his craving for glory. He is not sane."

That, of course, is an outright lie.

---

[39] In "The City on the Edge of Forever", *Star Trek: The Original Series* (S1/E28)

[40] In "The Enterprise Incident", *Star Trek: The Original Series* (S3/E2)

But these are exceptions that prove the rule. It takes a top-secret Starfleet espionage mission or a reality-bending timeline disaster to spur Kirk and Spock to outright falsehood.

The importance of integrity

It is disheartening to live in an era when falsehood and intentional disinformation is not only ubiquitous, but fast becoming the rule. Three decades into the Internet and 15 years into the era of social media, we *expect* to be lied to constantly – even (and especially) by our leaders. We factor deceit into nearly even communication.

If we're to be successful in pushing back against rising authoritarianism, we must build our worldview on positive, constructive agency in a world we feel responsible for improving. Lies and misinformation do not aid or promote that agency or improvement; they are gross impediments to it. To resist the authoritarian, then, is to commit to integrity and truth in all one's actions and dealings, even though it means a dispirited slog through a daily morass of ugly falsehood.

Humanists are quick to publicly proclaim this commitment:

"We believe in the common moral decencies: altruism, integrity, honesty, truthfulness, responsibility," reads Paul Kurtz's "A Statement of Principles" in Free Inquiry's *Affirmations of Humanism*. "Humanist ethics is amenable to critical, rational guidance. There are normative standards that we discover together. Moral principles are tested by their consequences."

"We believe in optimism rather than pessimism," he continues, "hope rather than despair, learning in the place of dogma, truth instead of ignorance, joy rather than guilt or sin, tolerance in the place of fear, love instead of hatred, compassion over selfishness, beauty instead of ugliness, and reason rather than blind faith or irrationality."

Scientific integrity as the model for truth

Committing to a non-magical, unwishful reality supported not only by the evidence of the senses but a foundation of sober reason leads many, if not most, into harmony with the method and findings of science. Empirical truth is generally accepted as the baseline for *all* truth; or, phrased antithetically, information or knowledge parading as truth that does *not* stand up to reason or empirical scrutiny is by its very nature suspect and likely to be rejected out of hand.

Humanists are not shy about stating this acceptance of science and its methods as truth-seeking. "Humanists embrace science as the most effective tool in understanding our reality," according to Andrew Copson. "Science values truth and looks for disagreement and debate to approach the truth more closely."

The American Humanist Association has formalized this embrace:

"The AHA considers the integrity of scientific knowledge, where information is assigned a degree of certainty according to the weight of the evidence, to be essential to a humanist society," it proclaims in its statement on Scientific Integrity.

"Humanists insist that scientific studies, peer-reviewed and reproduced in accordance with the highest standards, be the basis for public policy and education. Religious or sectarian doctrine is irrelevant and immaterial to discerning best practices."

It's worth a brief recap to remind ourselves exactly what this commitment entails.

Per the scientific method, for a new idea or theory to be accepted as fact, it must

- be thoroughly examined in an objective manner;

- be dispassionately tested via a method that can reveal its potential falsity;
- be subjected to intensive efforts to disprove it;
- endure repeated testing by others, to validate the correctness of its analysis

Then, and only then, can this new idea or information be accepted as fact.

Again, antithetically, the proclamations of those in authority do not become factual just because they are spoken by those in authority (this discounts almost everything offered by our current leaders).

The knowledge of the masses, no matter how universally embraced, isn't real knowledge solely on the basis of their broad acceptance.

And new ideas do not become credible or worthy of designation of fact simply because they are exciting, intriguing, or emotionally pleasing.

This means that new information we want to take on board as real must not only run the gauntlet of scientific scrutiny, but must swim upstream through the yowls of the crowd, the bellowing of the powerful and our own susceptibility to wishful thinking.

The humanist's attitude toward truth then, can be summed up as follows: you gotta want it bad, because the information streams of our current society are gonna put up a fight.

But humanists *do* want it bad. The humanist treasures truth and integrity, and science was invented explicitly to deliver them. Here are some excerpts from the American Humanist Association's Resolution on Scientific Integrity:

WHEREAS the power for human progress resident in modern science, when used and controlled democratically, offers a method for the establishment of peace on a global scale;

WHEREAS the outcomes of our actions are predicted by scientific methods and play a key role in our ethical decisions;

WHEREAS scientific leaders require the professional integrity to identify a level of certainty to all claims, distinguishing between tentative and conclusive findings;

BE IT RESOLVED in furtherance of human flourishing, the American Humanist Association

AFFIRMS that the methods of science be relied upon in assessing the efficacy of our actions and policies to bring about stated ethical outcomes;

AFFIRMS that a skeptical approach to knowledge, assigning a level of certainty according to the weight of the evidence, is important to personal well being;

DECRIES the elevation of ideological conviction or preconceived certainty over coherent theory, empirical observation, or expert peer review as determiners of truth;

DECRIES censorship, misinformation campaigns, and obstruction in the general populace, the Internet, or schools that subvert the process of free inquiry, dissemination of knowledge, or discovery of new information;

AFFIRMS that the advancement of scientific exploration and study must be tempered by humility, compassion, and constant care for all life and our environment.

We can easily imagine a species- and technology-agnostic version of this resolution hanging in the Daystrom Institute, or Starfleet Headquarters, or the Vulcan Science Academy.

Scientific truth, historical truth, personal truth

When Picard dresses Wesley down in the scene referenced above, he does us the favor of clarifying that *truth is truth* – every flavor of it, starting with objective science and weaving through the human story right down to our very subjective selves, clings unwaveringly to the same very high standards. It is particularly poignant for us, the viewers, that he takes the trouble to make this clarification, for we live in a world where scientific truths are just one-of-many, historical truths exist at the whims of the winners, and personal truth is anything-goes.

Not so Starfleet, or Roddenberry's future – or the here-and-now of the humanist. Truth and integrity are not subject to whim; they do not indulge our wishes and wants; and they are certainly not in the purview of the powerful. Truth and integrity are non-negotiable. They are precious, and like anything we greatly prize, they are of tremendous value and ask of us a dear price.

It's a price we must willingly pay – an essential part of our resistance.

"Leave any bigotry in your quarters. There's no room for it on the bridge!"

Racism and Social Inequality

"It is obvious to the most simple-minded that Lokai is of an inferior breed! All of his people are white on the right side!"
~Cheronian Commissioner Bele

In 1953 New York City, a science fiction writer named Benny Russell writes a story about a future interstellar space station called *Deep Space Nine*, where beings from many different worlds can be found. The commander of this space station is black, like Benny himself. He submits his story to Douglas Pabst, the editor of the science fiction magazine for which he writes.

Pabst rejects Benny's story, because it is believed that readers will recoil at the idea of a black commanding officer (Benny himself, and Kay – a female writer who writes under a gender-neural pseudonym – are excluded from staff photos so as not to alienate readers). Benny compromises with Pabst, rewriting the story so that it is represented as just a dream.

The revised story is rejected by the magazine's publisher, who instructs Pabst to fire Benny.

"You're firing me?" Benny asks, stunned.

"I have no choice, Benny," Pabst replies. "It's his decision." Benny explodes.

"I am a human being, damn it!" he shouts, in front of the entire staff (who are on his side). "You can deny me all you want but you cannot deny Ben Sisko. He exists! That future, that space station, all those people, they exist in here! In my mind, I created it! And every one of you know it. You read it. It's here! You hear what I'm telling you? You can pulp a story, but you cannot destroy an idea! Don't you understand? That's ancient knowledge. You cannot destroy an idea! That future, I created it, and it's real. Don't you understand? It is real! I created it and it's real! It's real!"[41]

Kirk and the *Enterprise* find themselves hosts to two humanoids from the non-aligned planet Cheron, where the inhabitants are white on one side and black on the other. Bele, a Cheronian official, has been pursuing Lokai, whom he identifies as a fugitive criminal, from planet to planet. Lokai's counter-claim is that he is a revolutionary, fighting for people who are oppressed by the government Bele represents.[42]

Caught in the middle, Kirk and Spock meet with Bele, struggling to understand. What is the conflict really about?

"It is obvious to the most simple-minded that Lokai is of an

---

[41] In "Far Beyond the Stars", *Star Trek: Deep Space Nine* (S6/E13)

[42] In "Let That Be Your Last Battlefield", *Star Trek: The Original Series* (S3/E15)

inferior breed," Bele explains.

"The obvious visual evidence, Commissioner," Spock replies, "is that he is of the same breed as yourself."

Bele is aghast.

"Are you blind, Commander Spock? Well, look at me! Look at me!"

"You're black on one side and white on the other," Kirk observes.

"I am black on the *right* side," Bele clarifies.

Kirk is baffled. "I fail to see the significant difference."

"Lokai is *white* on the right side! *All of his people are white on the right side!*"

On *Deep Space 9*, the Bajoran Major Kira arrests a visiting Cardassian, Marritza, believing him to be one of the soldiers from a labor camp, Gallitep, where Bajorans were abused and murdered by the Cardassians. Under interrogation, he confesses that he was at Gallitep, but was merely a file clerk. Investigating this, the station's personnel come across a photo that implicates Marritza as actually being the war criminal Gul Darhe'el, the "Butcher of Gallitep", long thought dead.[43]

When the Cardassian military assures Commander Sisko that Darhe'el is most certainly dead, it comes out that Marritza really *was* just a file clerk at Gallitep, but that he has been haunted in the years since by his memories of "those horrible screams! I covered my ears every night! You have no idea what it's like to be a coward, to see those horrors and do nothing!" Marritza's deliberate planting of suspicion that he is actually Darhe'el, to bring down justice upon himself by

---

[43] In "Duet", Star Trek: Deep Space Nine (S1/E19)

playing the role of the butcher, is an attempt at atonement.

Kira, letting go of her own bigotry, releases him, but another Bajoran stabs Marritza to death on the Promenade moments later:

"Why? He wasn't Darhe'el! Why?"

"He's a Cardassian! That's reason enough!"

"No... it's not..."

Star Trek's stand against racism and social inequality may be the most overt of its many woke stances. Instances of bigotry, when featured as story points, stand out in high relief for their contrast to the mores and principles of Roddenberry's Federation and Starfleet.

So prominent are these that *Trek* can even be accused of heavy-handedness in this regard, as in the scene from the original series episode "Let That Be Your Last Battlefield" cited above. Over the decades, *Trek*'s commentary on the toxicity of bigotry has been persistent and at times inventive (as in the DS9 "Far Beyond the Stars", also cited above).

Racism and humanism

It began with a scene in the original series first-season episode "Balance of Terror", when the crew of Kirk's *Enterprise* learns that the Romulans, who have never been seen before, are Vulcanoid – descended from ancestors in common with Spock's. Encountering a Romulan ship and noting that its crew strongly resemble Vulcans, Navigator Styles concludes that Spock himself could be a Romulan spy, and proceeds to indulge this ethnic ugliness by openly regarding him with increasing suspicion.

"Well, here's one thing you can be sure of, mister," Kirk reprimands him, "Leave any bigotry in your quarters. There's no room for it on the bridge. Do I make myself clear?"

Racism and social inequality have been with us for millennia, of course; even the holy texts of the major ancient religions are
teeming with it. They are such a human constant that it's easy to assume that they are built into human nature.

Gene Roddenberry didn't see it that way. In his formulation, racism and social inequality are social phenomena, not natural phenomena. In this, he was showing his emerging humanist ideals, and humanism has much to say about these issues.

It can be safely said that there are no humanist organizations today that have not publicly renounced bigotry, racism, and other prejudicial behaviors, and to denounce instances of social inequality wherever they may be found.

Here are some examples:

"The principle of moral equality must be furthered
through elimination of all discrimination based upon
race, religion, sex, age, or national origin. This means
equality of opportunity and recognition of talent and
merit. Individuals should be encouraged to contribute
to their own betterment. ... We deplore racial,
religious, ethnic, or class antagonisms. Although we
believe in cultural diversity and encourage racial and
ethnic pride, we reject separations which promote
alienation and set people and groups against each
other; we envision an integrated community where
people have a maximum opportunity for free and
voluntary association.

"At the present juncture of history, commitment to all
humankind is the highest commitment of which we
are capable; it transcends the narrow allegiances of
church, state, party, class, or race in moving toward a
wider vision of human potentiality. What more daring

a goal for humankind than for each person to become, in ideal as well as practice, a citizen of a world community."

~Eleventh Principle, Humanist Manifesto II

And this, from Humanists UK:

"Humanists condemn racism and racial discrimination in all its forms and are committed to campaigning for racial equality across all aspects of society. We have a positive track record throughout our existence in the fight for racial equality, from organising the first global race congress in 1911, to campaigning against colonialism in the early twentieth century, and for laws against racial discrimination from the mid-century. This commitment has continued through to today."

~Human Rights and Equality statement

And these excerpts from the Resolution on White Supremacy (American Humanist Association):

"*WHEREAS* white supremacy and the racism that sustains it remain particularized and systemic in our society, and

WHEREAS racism continues to limit the opportunities of and discriminate against racialized bodies of color in particular and marginalized bodies more generally, living in the United States by perpetuating inequality in every facet of individual and community life, and

WHEREAS hate crimes and hate groups have become more prevalent in the United States in recent years, especially targeting Black people, people perceived as Muslim, Jews, South Asians, LGBTQ people, and the disability community, and

WHEREAS dismantling white supremacy requires anti-racist action.

THEREFORE, BE IT RESOLVED that the AMERICAN HUMANIST ASSOCIATION, in the pursuit of an anti-racist society,

AFFIRMS that all lives will matter when Black lives matter, and

AFFIRMS that economic justice for Black and Indigenous people requires federal policies that take drastic corrective measures to eradicate the racial wealth gap, and

AFFIRMS its support for anti-racist healthcare, including mental health services, that achieves the same health outcomes for Black and White people regardless of income, and

AFFIRMS its dedication to stamping out white supremacy and racism from within its organization through hiring practices, resource allocation, staff and board training, and more.

Per the humanist dynamic, it is of course not enough to take a political or philosophical position on racism; humanism calls for individual commitment and action. To that end, Samuel Kronen in "A Plea for a Humanist Antiracism" (in *Aero*, 2020) spells out some specifics:

> "A humanist antiracism would reject all racial double standards and express equal opprobrium at the police killings of both George Floyd and Tony Timpa. It would acknowledge the brutal legacy of historical racism, as well as the astounding racial progress made in the past half century, while never losing sight of how much further we have to go before race is irrelevant in public life. It would condemn racism in the strongest possible terms and root out what

remains of it in our institutions, without suggesting that racism is responsible for everything that's unfair in society. It would reject notions of intergenerational bloodguilt and retributive justice. It would strive for a race-blind world without
ignoring instances of persistent racial injustice. It would create more breathing room for conversations about race, by allowing us to see each other as human beings and not simply as avatars of our races. It would appreciate the real advantages and disadvantages experienced by certain groups and individuals in society without making a religion out of the notion of privilege. It would reject the tendency to make meaning out of race and use race as a proxy for underlying social conditions. It would focus on hard policy reform over symbolic gestures of piety. It would measure progress by comparing metrics of well-being to those of the past rather than in terms of racial disparities. And it would reject systematic discrimination, whether in the form of overt racial quota systems in job applications and admissions procedures or subtle biases against blacks and other groups in policing, medicine and other sectors of American life."

Kronen's emphasis on social justice as the moving part in anti-racist action is echoed throughout the humanist communities and organizations of the world. Here's what the AHA says about it:

"Humanists are naturally committed to social justice as a prerequisite to peace and happiness for the greatest number and see it as a moral failing to stand by while others are denied their civil and human rights. Humanistic social justice advocacy involves respect for the equality of all people, compassion for their dignity and welfare, and a conviction that positive change requires human intervention.

"The AHA takes an intersectional view of social justice issues, recognizing that working to liberate all marginalized communities is the best way to lift the prospects of any one group. Humanism motivates us to act on a moral imperative to transform systems of oppression because they are incompatible with the aspirations of humanism.

"Regardless of race, ethnicity, economic status, ability, sexual orientation, gender identity, religious beliefs or nonbelief, or citizenship, all individuals have universal human rights that must be respected and protected. Achieving global standards for human rights and international adherence to institutions such as the International Criminal Court and the United Nations Universal Declaration of Human Rights facilitate enforcing individuals' rights the world over."

Racism today

In the US today, racism and social inequality have been on the rise, as right-wing politicians stir the animosities of white America with divisive rhetoric. Systemic racism has existed throughout the nation's existence, and social/economic inequality was the persistent companion of that racism until the 1950s. The Civil Rights Movement produced some gains – there are now black millionaires, black CEOs, even a black president – and access to higher education is now much easier for members of all ethnicities.

But there is still far to go. In a recent study conducted by Harvard's T.H. Chan School of Public Health, 57% of black Americans reported discrimination in pay and eligibility for promotion; 54% of Native Americans reported facing discrimination in hiring, promotion, and compensation.

The National Urban League reported in its 2022 annual report that, per the Equality Index, black Americans are only getting 73% as much of the American pie as white Americans; a black child born today can expect a life four years shorter, on average, than a white child; black women are 59% more likely to die while bearing a child than white women; 31% are more likely to die of breast cancer; black men are 52% more likely to die of prostate cancer.

According to a 2019 study by the Pew Research Center, 58% of Americans believe that racism in the nation is serious, and 56% believe that the Trump presidency made it worse. 51% of Americans believe that being Hispanic hinders a person's ability to succeed in the US. Among blacks themselves, 78% do not think enough has been done to address systemic racism in the US.

Regarding the expression of racist opinions and insensitive views, 65% of Americans believe that expression became more common after Donald Trump became president; 45% said it has become more acceptable.

Among white Democrats, 64% say they do not believe the nation has done enough to address systemic racism; among white Republicans, the number is 15%. 80% of white Democrats say the legacy of slavery continues to impact American society today, while only 40% of white Republicans feel the same. And 78% of white Democrats say the problem is people not seeing racism where it exists, while the same percentage of white Republicans say that people see racial discrimination where it really isn't.

These numbers give us the same feeling we get when we

watch "Let That Be Your Last Battlefield," don't they?

How we get Woke

Humanities Professor Anthony Pinn of Rice University gets more specific still, offering a list of Dos and Don'ts for the individual humanist to apply when actively confronting racism:[2]

- **Don't make blanket statements concerning African-American involvement in theism.** "The relationship between African-Americans and Christianity is complex and layered," Pinn points out; in the African-American past, it pushed against injustice and helped produce a sense of identity and agency that worked against the dehumanization they were experiencing.

- **Don't assume humanism is a vaccine against poor thinking and poor behavior.** Humanists, Pinn asserts, are cultural creatures, and can be insensitive to racial injustice through the simple mechanism of believing that the logic they embrace elevates them beyond it.

- **Don't assume you get to set the racial justice agenda.** "You don't get to determine what are appropriate markers of progress," Pinn writes; "your job is to promote solidarity, and to play the role assigned to you by those who are most directly and deeply impacted by issues of race and racism."

- **Do recognize the nature of privilege.** "Whiteness" comes with perks, Pinn states. There are forms of privilege that lurk in the background, to which the humanist should be alert: the assumption that the police are there to serve and protect, for instance, and the assumption that you weren't placed near the restroom in the restaurant because of the color of your skin.

- **Do educate yourself.** The serious humanist should put the same energy into learning about matters of race, Pinn insists, that they put toward learning about separation of church and state, evolution, and other important humanist issues.
- **Do recognize difference as an opportunity.** Difference, per Pinn, is "an opportunity... a chance to add complexity to a community and to learn from approaches and perspectives outside what is considered normative. It's an opportunity to appreciate what has been considered marginal to U.S. life and to understand its actual centrality. In a certain way, difference as opportunity points to the need to appreciate cultural diversity, learn from it, and embrace possibilities that push us beyond the familiar and comfortable."

All pretty Woke, isn't it?

We can give Gene Roddenberry himself the last word on this one:

> "We must learn to live together," he says *The Making of Star Trek*, with a touch of civil rights and Cold War concerns, "or most certainly we will soon all die together."

LGBTQ

"I love her, Benjamin."

"I know you do. If I were in your position, I'd probably be

just as ready to throw everything away for the person I love. But I would also want to be sure that I was ready to pay the price."

~Jadzia Dax and Benjamin Sisko

Picard's *Enterprise* assists the J'naii, who are not members of the Federation, in locating a missing spacecraft. Riker, piloting a shuttle to rescue the J'naii ship when it's found, meets Soren, who offers to co-pilot. Soren is androgynous, and as they become acquainted, Riker realizes that all J'naii are; the expression of a gender preference is not permitted in J'naii society.[44]

When Soren is injured, she is treated by Dr. Crusher, and inquires about female gender identify. She is attracted to Riker, and reveals that she has an unexpressed female identity. This is considered a

perversion among the J'naii, and those who make such expressions are subjected to "psychotectic therapy" to remove their gender specificity. If they do not submit, they are cast out.

When Soren's feelings for Riker are discovered, she is put on trial, and will not permit Riker to intervene for her (and which Picard will not permit either, because Prime Directive). When he returns to her world and tries to rescue her, it's too late; she has been subjected to the therapy already, and now considers herself "normal".

Jadzia Dax of *Deep Space 9* is a Trill – a joined species, consisting of a humanoid host and an implanted lifeform with

---

[44] In "The Outcast", *Star Trek: The Next Generation* (S5/17)

its own intelligent consciousness. Trill host and symbiont remain joined until the host humanoid dies, at which time the symbiont is implanted in a new host, retaining its memories from all its joined identities. The symbiont, then, can potentially live centuries. It can also be moved from a male humanoid body into a female one, and vice versa, and over eight humanoid lifetimes, Dax has alternated between genders.[45]

When a Trill science team arrives at *DS9*, it turns out that one of them – Lenara Kahn – was once Dax's wife. Captain Sisko realizes the implication of this, as Trill are not supposed to reassociate with former partners, and offers Dax a leave of absence, but she refuses.

Becoming reacquainted in new humanoid bodies – both female – Dax and Kahn recall their hosts from their time as a married couple. They warm to one another, and their feelings are rekindled. Acting on those feelings, however, would get them banished from Trill society, and they would not be permitted new hosts. When Dax tells Sisko about their renewed relationship, he offers his support, but before things go further Kahn is injured in an accident – and, reminded of the fragility of life and the consequences of the loss of access to a new host if either of them are mortally injured, she breaks off her relationship with Dax and departs with the other Trill.

Believing he has solved a key piece of his creator's process for building a positronic brain, Data resolves to create his own offspring. He does so, building an android like himself. He crafts his offspring's body to be slightly smaller than his own,

---

[45] In "Rejoined", *Star Trek: Deep Space Nine* (S4/E6)

appearing more or less as a teenager, but does not assign it a gender.[46]

Once his offspring (whom he names Lal – Hindi for "beloved") is activated and conscious, he offers it whatever appearance it desires. Though he himself is male – *completely male* – he makes no assumptions about his new child's gender identity, allowing it to come to that awareness on its own. It – she – realizes she is female, and Data provides her with an appropriate appearance.

In the Right's War on Woke, there are few issues as venomous as sexual orientation. People who don't conform to a white, Christian view of the bedroom seem to make them disturbingly uncomfortable.

This is no surprise. Long before the word "woke" came along – long before "conservative" and "liberal" became sociopolitical designations – authoritarian and patriarchal personalities have bristled and howled over people who do not conform to their notions of correct and proper sexuality. We don't have to look further than the Old Testament to realize this way of thinking has been with us for thousands of years.

This does not fully explain, however, the anti-Woke crowd's laser-sharp targeting of LGBTQ people at this particular moment in history. So intense has these attacks become that they echo the Right's war on the environment: they despise pro-LGBTQ policy so deeply that they vigorously assault businesses who deploy it – even though the pro-LGBTQ policies are good for business, and (on paper) they themselves are pro-

---

[46] In "The Offspring", *Star Trek: The Next Generation* (S3/E16)

business.

Here are some examples:

- Per a report in *Forbes*, when Woolworths tweeted support for International Pride Month, expressing commitment to their LGBTQ customers, conservative outrage ensued; Woolworth's doubled down, tweeting that "every person has the right to dignity, regardless of their identity; this is a fact enshrined in our constitution, it is not up for debate";
- Similar conservative outrage erupted in New Zealand, when The Warehouse retail outlet sold items from the Disney pride collection;
- More of the outrage emerged over *Glamour UK*, which featured a picture of pregnant transgender man Logan Broan on its cover;
- According to the *Dallas Morning News*, Southwest Airlines has been forced to deal with a website and local billboard smearing it as "Southwoke" for its promotion of racial and LGBTQ diversity;
- Target bowed to similar anti-Woke pressure, pulling LGBTQ items from its Pride collection when workers' safety was threatened, according to the *Washington Post*;
- The *New York Times* reported that Anheuser-Busch made a similar retreat in the face of conservative boycotts following TikTok star Dylan Mulvaney's promotion of a beer contest; two of the company's top executives were put on leave, and the company announced that its future marketing would focus on sports and music.

"Recent pushback against businesses such as Anheuser-

Busch and Target, blatantly organized by extremist groups, serves as a wake up call for all businesses that support the LGBTQ+ community," read a statement from the Human Rights Campaign. "We've seen this extremist playbook of attacks before. Their goal is clear: to prevent LGBTQ+ inclusion and representation, silence our allies and make our community invisible."

As with the rage over businesses treating the environment responsibly, this behavior makes no economic sense: the asset management group LGBT Capital estimates that the annual purchasing power of the global LGBTQ community is $3.9 trillion. No business in its right mind would turn its back on such a broad customer base.

It's not just the assault on business; worse than that is the assault on law.

The Republican governor of Florida, Ron DeSantos, has become the public face of the anti-LGBTQ Right, with two major bills that have received national attention and scrutiny: an "anti-woke" bill and the "Don't Say Gay" bill. Both are designed to dictate what teachers can and cannot say in classrooms. The first presents a list of race-related concepts that are forbidden in lessons for students; the second prohibits discussion of sexual orientation and gender identity in grade school classrooms. The irony in the latter case, of course, is that teachers were not presenting those topics to children of that age in the first place, suggesting that the law is pure political posturing.

At the federal level, anti-LGBTQ legislation has been surfacing in must-pass funding bills in the House of Representatives, with Republican lawmakers embedding 45 such provision in those bills in an attempt to weaken discrimination protections for same-sex couples and restrict gender-affirming care. Several appropriations bills include provisions for the restriction of gender transition care for those on Medicare, Medicaid, and ACA-subsidized plans. They would also impact trans members of the military and their dependents, as well as federal employees. There are also provisions for the banning of Pride flags over government buildings, the nullification of protections for same-sex couples, and restriction of funding of programs promoting diversity and inclusion.

Down in Texas, the Republican Party has formally defined homosexuality as an "abnormal lifestyle choice" and openly stated its opposition to "all efforts to validate transgender identity." The party platform includes a call to repeal the 1965 Voting Rights Act, as well as a statement that LGBTQ people should not be legally protected from discrimination. It further states that being gay or trans is a choice.

"We believe there should be no granting of special legal entitlements or creation of special status for homosexual behavior, regardless of state of origin, and we oppose any criminal or civil penalties against those who oppose homosexuality out of faith, conviction, or belief in traditional values," it reads.

Texas Republicans have also called for a ban on gender-affirming care.

In 2022, more than 300 anti-LGBTQ bills were pending in state legislatures. According to the Human Rights Campaign, at least six states have banned transgender women and girls from competing on sports teams consistent with their gender. Alabama, Arizona and Texas have taken steps to ban gender-affirming care for young people; in Alabama, it is now a felony for a doctor to provide such care to minors. Other states are also following Florida's lead, introducing bills that mimic "Don't Say Gay".

Three states now have laws in place preventing trans children from accessing care for gender dysphoria, even when recommended by major medical associations. Two have outlawed discussion of LGBTQ history or individuals in classrooms.

And then there are the Christians...

Randall Balmer, a professor at Dartmouth who grew up in an Evangelical household, offers some perspective on the breathtaking surge in LGBTQ hatred, noting that much of it comes from Evangelicals. The point of it all, he has written, is to keep that community mobilized as a voting block for the Right.[1]

"They have an interest in keeping the base riled up about one thing or another, and when one issue fades, as with same-sex relationships and same-sex marriage, they've got to find something else," Balmer said in an interview with *The 19th*. "It's almost frantic."

His research traces this methodology to Paul Weyrich, one of the founders of the Religious Right, in the Seventies. Weyrich began testing issues that would drive Evangelicals to the voting booth, and this became a standard practice, permanently installing white Evangelicals as the key factor in Republican wins.

Once gay marriage was settled, much to the Religious Right's chagrin, "they almost frantically began looking for something else," Balmer said. "And of course, the trans thing was the next thing on the horizon."

What the public thinks

What does the general public think of all this? Unsurprisingly, there's a clear partisan divergence: 3/4[th]s of Republicans say the US should promote traditional values, and 2/3[rd]s of Democrats support greater tolerance of diversity. Independents are split down the middle.

That poll gets more granular, asking very specific questions about tolerance from a public policy viewpoint:

- Government should promote greater respect for traditional values: 27% (D), 65% (R)
- Government should promote greater tolerance of people with different lifestyles: 66% (D), 18% (R)
- US should increase social justice: 66% (D), 21% (R)
- The country should reduce political correctness and cancel culture: 19% (D), 67% (R)
- Promotion of LGBTQ lifestyle and values has gone too far: 12% (D), 70% (R)
- The US should be more accepting of the LGBTQ community: 60% (D), 10% (R)

US voters across the political spectrum acknowledge that the surge in anti-LGBTQ legislation is political theater more than moral conviction. In a 2023 Data for Progress survey, those who think there is "too much" legislation aimed at "limiting the rights of transgender and gay people in America" include 64% of voters in general; 72% of Democrats, 65% of Independents, and 55% of Republicans.

General support for marriage equality is now around 70%, with PRRI's 2022 American Values Atlas noting that same-sex marriage support is at 60% or greater in 43 states.

Per the non-partisan Public Religion Research Institute, almost 80% of Americans support protections against discrimination for LGBTQ people (this even includes 65% of Republicans). A 2021 PBS Newshour/NPR/Marist poll reported that 2/3rds of Americans oppose bills that limit transgender rights.

We've already noted in the broader discussion of diversity above that our differences make human community stronger, an idea that *Trek* emphasized again and again. Increasing diversity and tolerance, and pushing back against attacks on both, is not only noble; it's a means of improving our collective capability and accelerating human progress. It is worthy of our deep commitment and investment.

The past few decades of American life have demonstrated what honest, self-aware people have known all along, and which our *Trek* heroes underscored over and over: skin color makes no difference; gender makes no difference. And neither does sexual orientation. It's as Woke *Trek* to support the LGBTQ community as it is to support racial and gender equality.

"When my status as a living being was in question, you fought to protect my rights, and for that I will always be grateful."

Rights and Freedoms

"Hear me! Hear this! Among my people, we carry many such words as this from many lands, many worlds. Many are equally good and are as well respected, but wherever we have gone, no words have said this thing of importance in quite this way. Look at these three words written larger than the rest, with a special pride never written before or since. Tall words, proudly saying 'We the People!' These words and the words that follow were not written only for the Yangs, but for the Kohms as well!

"The Kohms?"

"They must apply to everyone, or they mean nothing! Do you understand?"

~Kirk to Cloud William

Data risks the lives of Picard and best friend Geordi LaForge on Tyrus 7a, when a group of autonomous robots called Exocomps display evidence that they have evolved and become sentient, and he refuses to allow them to be ordered to their deaths in order to rescue Picard and LaForge.[47]

Picard and LaForge are rescued in the end, when the Exocomps voluntarily come to their aid. Data explains his actions to Picard:

"I thought you might want to know why I would be willing to risk your life for several small machines," Data says to Picard.

"I think I understand the predicament you were in. It could not have been an easy choice."

"No, sir, it was not," Data replies. "When my status as a living being was in question, you fought to protect my rights, and for that I will always be grateful. The Exocomps had no such advocate. If I had not acted in their behalf, they would have been destroyed. I could not allow that to happen, sir."

"Of course you couldn't," Picard agrees. "It was the most human decision you've ever made."

Pike's *Enterprise* intercepts and rescues an alien shuttle harboring a young boy, fleeing a non-Federation planet where he is presumably to be honored with the status of First Servant of his people. Pike and company are convinced by those pursuing the boy that he was being kidnapped, and that they are doing a good thing by returning him. Later, they learn that the boy's "Ascension" to the position of First Servant involves a ceremony where he is plugged into a vast machine, for life. This machine controls their society – and, in particular, it keeps their cities floating in the clouds, far above the unfriendly surface of the planet, which everyone very

---

47 In "The Quality of Life", *Star Trek: The Next Generation* (S6/E9)

much enjoys.[48]

Pike is horrified to learn that he has aided and abetted in bringing about this boy's monstrous fate. He confronts the woman who has been explaining it all to him.

"What did you do to that boy?"

"The Ascension is complete," she says, "You may go."

"You're damn right I'm going," Pike answers, "getting that child the hell away from that thing."

"Even if you could get into the Chamber, severing the connection would only kill him."

"Why?"

"Serving Majalis is his destiny. His reason for being."

"You plugged a kid into a machine. What's it gonna do to him?"

"We don't know," she shrugs. "The machine needs the neural network of a child to function. Our founders designed it that way. We don't know why. We've hunted for centuries for alternatives and found nothing. It was the purpose of my research when we met."

"Will he suffer?"

"Yes. We don't pretend otherwise. We live in gratitude for him. And when a new First Servant ascends, we will live for her."

"Your whole civilization," Pike rails in disgust, "all your – this. It's all founded on the suffering of a child... The first chance I get, I'm reporting this to Starfleet."

Most of the pushback against Woke is about rights – human rights, civil rights, political rights, economic rights, social

---

[48] Repeated, from above: In "Lift Us Where Suffering Cannot Reach", *Star Trek: Strange New Worlds* (S1/E6)

rights, cultural rights. If you're Woke, you generally believe that these rights, and the freedoms they enshrine, should be available to all; if you're not Woke, you generally believe that some people should have fewer rights than others.

The tendency of the anti-Woke to attack some specific groups – LGBTQ, for instance – is examined below. But the general pushback against equal rights for all exists over and above specific attacks on specific groups; it is founded on a belief, held by far too many, that some people are better or more worthy than others.

That belief flies in the face of democracy, of course; but the staggering depth of the chasm between the Woke view on rights and freedoms and the view of Woke's opposition is truly commitment to two separate realities.

> *"The basic tool for the manipulation of reality is the manipulation of words. If you can control the meaning of words, you can control the people who must use the words."*
>
> *~Philip K. Dick*

Philip K. Dick. Wouldn't it have been great if he'd written an episode of *Trek*?

The dual realities we find ourselves confronting is based on two completely different meanings of the word *freedom*.

The point of rights is to secure freedoms; attacks on the rights of any particular group are an attempt to restrict or remove that group's freedoms. Defense of those rights, conversely, are attempts to preserve those freedoms.

What freedoms are we talking about?

If you're Woke, those include freedom from persecution over sexual orientation, gender identity, skin color or ethnicity. You support equal rights for persons in these groups, and expect the government to enforce those rights. 'We the People', to you, means people of all colors, ethnic origins, religions, and sexual persuasions.

If you aren't, *freedom* doesn't mean rights shared by all, enforced by the government; it means freedom *from* government.

This idea has been in the US water supply for more than a century, but it took root in the public gestalt with the election of Ronald Reagan to the White House in 1980. It was a coup for a particular cabal of economists, politicians, and businessmen – disciples of *neoliberalism*.

Neoliberalism and freedom

The neoliberal agenda is vast, but its central tenets are easily summarized:

- The US government is your enemy;
- The government needs to get out of the business of helping average Americans;
- The well-being of business transcends the national interest;
- *Deregulate, deregulate, deregulate!*

Ronald Reagan was a neoliberal juggernaut on all these fronts, setting the tone and strategy for all in the GOP who would follow him.

His assaults on the democratic order weren't just systematic and persistent; they were overt, out in the open, often paraded on national television.

"Government is not the solution to our problem, government *is* the problem," he declared, followed later by, "The nine most terrifying words in the English language are: 'I'm from the government, and I'm here to help.'" – casually vilifying, at a stroke, the hundreds of thousands who *do* enter public service out of a deep desire and conviction to help others and contribute to the betterment of the nation.

Reagan's demonization of government, already a GOP staple, was perhaps the least of it; his valentine to capitalism, a gutting of tax policy that had been in place since World War II, requiring businesses and the very wealthy to contribute their fair share back to the economy that had enriched them, exploded the national debt. In cutting the top tax rate from 70% to 25%, he tripled that debt, from $738 billion to $2.4 trillion. That quickly, the US went from being the world's largest creditor to the world's largest debtor.

The justification was that the US economy wasn't functioning properly, but that wasn't true at all. The economy had boomed steadily during the post-World War II years, with only the normal fluctuations. The number of people in the US living in poverty had continually declined, even as the overall population rose.

In the process, Reagan and his allies laid track for the GOP to come by dissembling in the media to justify his agenda. His budget director, David Stockman, perpetuated the trickle-down gospel that cutting taxes on corporations and the wealthy would trigger large returns as the savings would be re-invested in the economy, in effect paying for the cuts. The Office of Management and Budget debunked this myth with actual analysis, prompting Stockman to confess publicly that "None of us really understands what's going on with all these numbers... the whole thing is premised on faith, on a belief about how the world works."

'Trickle-down' wasn't real economic theory; it was conservative, neoliberal ideology. And when Stockman later said publicly that the tax cuts really were, in fact, a valentine to business, calling the whole thing a 'Trojan horse', he was castigated by the president.

Forty years later, 'trickle-down' has yet to function as

promised, even though the current crop of GOP politicians continue to shop it; the money the uber-wealthy are saving on their tax bills isn't and never has been re-invested in the economy. It sits in off-shore accounts.

A firestorm of deregulation followed the tax cuts, stagnating the prosperity of the middle class as the growth of the minimum wage dropped away and economic inequality surged. The push for privatization of government began in earnest, sending healthcare costs into the stratosphere, and barriers to the exporting of US manufacturing to nations where labor was far cheaper evaporated. The export of US manufacturing to other countries, gutting the domestic jobs market as it dismantled unions, was accompanied by a breathtaking surge in the trade deficit. Reagan inherited from Carter a deficit of only $13 billion; when he left office, it had soared to a mind-blowing $685 billion.

Perhaps most damning was the elimination of the Fairness Doctrine in 1987. The policy that had protected the integrity of public information since the dawn of radio was dropped, enabling the wild-west, anything-goes parade of disinformation and outright deception that clogs up media today. The airwaves ceased to be conduits for news and became what they are today – ideology pipelines.

Neoliberalism was off and running. The global, regulation-free landscape for the cultivation of wealth envisioned by Milton Friedman and his cohorts was finally taking shape. The transformation of the US government from the middle-class-building, consumer-protecting, civil-rights-promoting agency it had become since the New Deal into capitalism's passive enabler was well underway.

Reaganism was indeed a Trojan horse, and the forces it unleashed have ended or endangered many of the institutions we thought would last forever. Civil discourse in the conducting of the people's business is long gone; inequality has surged; people no longer trust those they count on to protect them. Deceit has been normalized, the rule of law is precarious, and violence – even murder! – in pursuit of political ends is becoming acceptable on US soil.

All so Elon Musk can go to Mars.

Born in the South

Historian Heather Cox Richardson reminds us that this way of thinking goes back to the Civil War: the precursor to modern neoliberalism was the slave trade of the 19th century South, and the wealthy men who enabled it:[1]

"The Thirteenth Amendment abolished human enslavement in the United States, except as punishment for a crime (an exception that later enabled the use of chain gangs). President Abraham Lincoln and the congressmen who embraced this monumental change to the Constitution expected that ending enslavement would end the power of a few elite southerners to dismantle the United States.

"Enslavement, they believed, had enabled a few men to monopolize wealth and power in the American South, where they dominated state governments and wrote laws to protect their own interests. Those same men had taken over first the Democratic Party and then the national government, controlling the Supreme Court, the Senate, and the presidency.

"The elite southerners insisted that the national government had no power to do anything that was not spelled out in the Constitution. It could protect the property interests of enslavers - through a law forcing free states to return escaped slaves, for example, or

laws protecting enslavement in the western territories
- but it
could not do anything to help ordinary Americans,
like dredging harbors, building roads, or establishing
colleges, no matter how popular those measures
might be.

"During the Civil War, Lincoln and his party rejected
this old formula and created a new one. They
pioneered a government that responded to the
interests of ordinary Americans. Amending the
Constitution to end enslavement was not simply an
attempt to guarantee freedom for Black Americans; it
was also designed to cement in place the government
'of the people, by the people, for the people.'

"Demonstrating that momentous change, the second
section of the Thirteenth Amendment added:
'Congress shall have power to enforce this article by
appropriate legislation.' The first ten amendments to
the Constitution - the Bill of Rights - limited the
power of the federal government. The Thirteenth was
the first to expand it.

"[Lincoln and his supporters] knew that Black
southerners supported this new government. They
believed that poorer white southerners who had been
crushed economically before the war as wealthy white
enslavers gobbled up the region's best land and who
had borne the brunt of the war would also embrace it.
Under the new system, the North had defied all
expectations and thrived during the war, and they
thought its superiority to the old system was so
obvious that ordinary southerners would jump at it.

"Many did... but white lawmakers in the southern

states did not. They agreed to ratify the Thirteenth
Amendment, but enabled by President Andrew
Johnson,
who took over the presidency after Lincoln's
assassination, they passed a series of laws that bound
Black Americans to yearlong contracts working in
white-owned fields, prohibited Black Americans from
meeting together or owning guns, demanded that
Black Americans behave submissively to white
Americans, and sometimes punished white people
who interacted with their Black neighbors.

"The *Chicago Tribune* wrote, 'The men of the North
will turn the State of Mississippi into a frog-pond
before they will allow any such laws to disgrace one
foot of soil in which the bones of our soldiers sleep
and over which the flag of freedom waves.' To counter
these 'Black Codes,' Congress wrote the Fourteenth
Amendment in 1866, and the states ratified it in 1868.

"Congress designed the Fourteenth Amendment to
end forever the ability of state lawmakers to
undermine the United States of America. The
amendment declared anyone born or naturalized in
the United States to be a U.S. citizen and then
established the power of the federal government to
stop states from discriminating against citizens. The
Fourteenth Amendment establishes that states must
treat everyone equally before the law, and they can't
take away someone's rights without due process of the
law."

The Civil War, then, provides us with a mirror in which to
view our situation today: to the Woke North, *freedom* meant

freedom for both white and black; to the anti-Woke South (the wealthy slaveowners, anyway), *freedom* meant *freedom from the*
federal government's interference in our right to take away the freedom of black people.

'Twas ever thus. The Woke struggle is just another expression of a conflict that has burdened humankind since the invention of the idea of property: some believe they are more equal than others – and the wealthy, in particular, have been the ones to seize power whenever possible to secure their wealth by trimming away the power, rights, and freedoms of those others.

Operation Iraqi Freedom?

In another modern example, part of the Right's rhetoric over the conquest of Iraq in 2003 was that the invasion would democratize that nation – restore *freedom* to the Iraqi people. When President George Bush announced the invasion on March 19, 2003, he put a name to it: Operation Iraqi Freedom.

It's hard to imagine a greater irony, even from him.

"A peaceful world of growing freedom," Bush wrote on the first anniversary of 9/11, "serves American long-term interests, reflects enduring American ideals and unites America's allies. Humanity holds in its hands the opportunity to offer freedom's triumph over all its age-old foes... as the greatest power on Earth, we have an obligation to help the spread of freedom."

Reading those words, the average American would assume Bush meant we were invading Iraq to spread equal rights, to ensure the freedoms of all its citizens, regardless of their religion, color, sexual orientation, and so on. Like in America.

But, no; the *freedom* we were spreading was *neoliberalism*.

In September of the same year, Paul Bremer, head of the Coalition Provisional Authority, produced a series of orders to be implemented in the new Iraq:

- The full privatization of public enterprises;
- Full ownership rights, by foreign firms, of Iraqi businesses;
- The opening of Iraq's banks to foreign control;
- The elimination of all trade barriers.

Put another way, Iraq was to be *deregulated*.

On the other hand, what *would* be regulated – and heavily so - would be Iraqi workers themselves:

- Strikes were effectively forbidden in key sectors;
- The right to unionize was heavily restricted;
- A regressive flat tax would be imposed.

Iraqi was not to be made a *free* state in the sense that most Americans understand the term; it was to be made a *neoliberal* state, one that existed under conditions friendly to neoliberal visions of global markets.

When we wrap our heads around this appropriation of words and the imposition of very different meanings, we more clearly understand the staggering distance between Woke thought and convictions, and the thought and convictions of those who oppose it.

Governance as incentive

Conservatives, and neoliberals in particular, want to shrink government to the point they can drown it because they believe government is only good for one thing: protecting their property. All its other functions, particularly social functions, should be eradicated.

As they say that, they profess to be all for human

flourishing, but that the *market* should be the source of that flourishing – not government.

The problem is, when people are flourishing, the wealthy can be counted on to find a way to exploit them. And the market can't do anything to stop them. Government is necessary to incentivize the proliferation of the freedoms that improve human well-being, because the market certainly doesn't; and, conversely, the government is necessary to *dis*-incentivize exploitation and the violation of the rights of others, by punishing those violations.

Other forces for Woke

We can imagine that the United Federation of Planets has a universal manifesto articulating the rights and freedoms of its citizens, and that these are enshrined somewhere for all to see. We have some similar codifications of our own.

The United Nations Universal Declaration on Human Rights

"Human rights include the right to life and liberty, freedom from slavery and torture, freedom of opinion and expression, the right to work and education, and many more. Everyone is entitled to these rights, without discrimination."

The UN specifies 30 basic human rights:

- All human beings are free and equal
- No discrimination
- Right to life
- No slavery
- No torture and inhuman treatment
- Same right to use law
- Equal before the law
- Right to treated fair by court
- No unfair detainment
- Right to trial
- Innocent until proved guilty
- Right to privacy
- Freedom to movement and residence
- Right to asylum
- Right to nationality
- Rights to marry and have family
- Right to own things
- Freedom of thought and religion
- Freedom of opinion and expression
- Right to democracy
- Right to social security
- Right to work
- Right to rest and holiday
- Right of social service
- Right to education
- Right of cultural and art
- Freedom around the world
- Subject to law
- Human rights can't be taken away

The International Covenant on Economic, Social, and Cultural

Rights (1976)

The human rights that the Covenant seeks to promote and protect include:

- the right to work in just and favourable conditions;
- the right to social protection, to an adequate standard of living and to the highest attainable standards of physical and mental well-being;
- the right to education and the enjoyment of benefits of cultural freedom and scientific progress.

Freedom House

"Democracy depends on the guarantee of equal rights under law and freedom from discrimination for all individuals in a society. If the rights and freedoms of one segment of the population are violated with impunity, the same sorts of abuses are likely to be visited on others. Those forced to endure a subordinate status have less incentive to play by the rules, creating a vicious circle of defiance and repression."

Woke knows where it stands, when it comes to rights. Freedoms. Woke stands with Kirk. With Picard. Pike. Data.

"The needs of the many outweigh the needs of the few."

Working for the Greater Good

The *Enterprise*, now a training vessel commanded by Spock, is en route to Regula I, a Federation research outpost where the Genesis Project is underway – and which the 20th century genetic warlord Khan is headed, in order to abscond with it. Kirk doesn't yet know what's going on, but he speaks to Spock about it in the latter's quarters. Spock offers to step aside and let Kirk take command of the ship.[49]

"It may be nothing," Kirk says. "Garbled communications. You take the ship."

"Jim, you proceed from a false assumption. I am a Vulcan. I have no ego to bruise."

"You're about to remind me that logic alone dictates your actions."

"I would not remind you of that which you know so well," Spock replies. "In any case, were I to invoke logic, logic clearly dictates that the needs of the many outweigh the needs of the few."

---

[49] In *Star Trek II: The Wrath of Khan*

"...or the one," Kirk adds.

Later, of course, this exchange – over nothing more consequential than who drives the bus – turns out to have been the foreshadowing of a much, much greater one-for-many sacrifice, as Spock lays down his life for his friends in their confrontation with Khan.

The practice of sacrificing for the greater good is not always this dramatic or momentous, of course; *Star Trek* framea up the 'greater good' in humbler terms, focusing more on the bedrock of social cooperation and mutual support between members of the community than upon life-or-death gestures. The idea is that each member of Federation society understands that the good of the community is ultimately everyone's highest priority; no one member is more important than any other, and all are committed to the greater good.

This mindset stands in opposition to the *Mad Men* world in which Gene Roddenberry was creating *Trek*, a world wherein each person is in it for themselves, first and foremost, and getting ahead of everyone else is the priority. This was especially true in the entertainment industry, where competition is everything and climbing to the top on the backs of others is commonplace.

Put another way, the *Star Trek* ethos is essentially anti-capitalist. And Roddenberry had no problem being very blunt about that.

"*Star Trek* showed us a future where diverse peoples come together across differences to work for the common good," said Gene's son Rod, years after his father's death, on the occasion of the creation of the Roddenberry Foundation. That organization, created in Gene's memory, undertakes projects that advance human progress and supports individuals and organizations pursuing social justice and equality.

The Greater Good

That mindset is a humanist mindset, through-and-through. Though it would be unfair to label the institution of humanism as anti-capitalist, it is certainly fair to say that the humanist views the greater good as a higher priority than personal wealth or success. The humanist is, by definition, on the side of humanity as a whole, rather than in competition with it.

"Humanism is a progressive philosophy of life that, without theism and other supernaturalism, affirms our ability and responsibility to lead ethical lives of personal fulfillment that aspire to the greater good of humanity," says the *Humanist Manifesto III* (2003).

"Humanists are everyday people who espouse the principles of humanism," according to the Humanist Society. "The principles of humanism include helping others, concern for our environment, meeting in community with others of like mind, making connections and growing by connection with others who hold diverse beliefs, and building a legacy that makes our world a better place."

Audrey Kingstrom, president of Humanists of Minnesota, said it like this:

"Unless one can believe in human agency. Own it. Claim it. Not just for oneself, but collectively for the greater good. That's what we must do as a humanist community. Ours is not merely a philosophy on paper. It's a lived experience. Of being our best selves. Living our best lives. And doing the most good that we can in the world. Spreading and sharing the world's good fortune that has graced our own lives.

"As humanists, we don't own the admonition to do good in the world. But we aren't doing it to save anyone's soul or to insure our own reward of heaven. We do it to ease suffering, to bring joy to another, to show compassion, to provide comfort. We do it because we can, because of our own good fortune – not out of fear or favor.

"We do it to spread a culture of goodness in the world because we know that even if we do not need it now for ourselves, a time will come when we will need it from others. We do it because we understand human frailty and connection. We do it because that is the kind of world we want to live in. One filled with kindness and compassion, civility, and equity. We do it because actions speak louder than words.

"Our good work together as humanists is essential if we are to make our mark on the world. Our service in the community and our advocacy in the public square matters. There is no justice and no goodness other than what we ourselves commit to each other and the world. That's humanism."

Pursuit of the Greater Good

An advantage humanism in practice can claim over other, similar good-of-all philosophies is its emphasis on that agency Kingstrom refers to above. There's a plan of action; there's an implicit requirement that comes with membership, a commitment to make the well-being of others and one's own actions a contribution to the general good that defines the humanist.

"Humanists are clear and certain that the social good, both in the present and future, should be the supreme ethical goal," writes Corliss Lamont in *The Philosophy of Humanism*. "That goal is inclusive of all humanity and envisages the on-going survival of the human race as inherently worthwhile. Logic alone will not win people's assent to the social good as the paramount aim in life; the desirability of that aim is not something that can be proved like a mathematical proposition. It is a vast ethical *assumption*, as important in its field as the scientific assumption of the Uniformity of Nature. Humanism consciously makes this ethical assumption, tries to persuade people in general to make it, and advocates the kind of education that will lead them to make it. Hence the humanist ethic urges the development of those basic impulses of love, friendliness, and cooperation that impel a person to consider constantly the good of the group and to find personal happiness in working for the happiness of all.

"As I have already pointed out, an individual's loyalty to their larger social good may under certain circumstances cost them their very existence or at least considerable suffering. We must frankly admit that a person's uncompromising dedication to the happiness of others may lead to unhappiness on their part. A pure conscience is not in itself sufficient to offset the persecution of governments or the cruelty of tyrants. As Aristotle sensibly observed in *The Nicomachean Ethics*: 'To assert that a person on the rack, or a person plunged in the depth of calamities, is happy is either intentionally or unintentionally to talk nonsense.' 'Virtue is its own reward' in the sense that the awareness of doing right always brings spiritual satisfaction; but such satisfaction is not sufficient to make the total person happy when they are suffering excruciating physical punishment. And if they are executed for their virtue, their 'reward' quickly comes to an end altogether.

"On the whole, however, a society in which most individuals, regardless of the personal sacrifices that may be entailed, are devoted to the collective well-being, will attain greater happiness and make more progress than one in which private self-interest and advancement are the prime motivation."

Lamont's framing here is eloquent, and noteworthy for its frankness; he does not shy away from the downside of self-subordination, and is honest about the possible consequences of sacrifice for the greater good.

He also does us the service, in *The Philosophy of Humanism*, of outlining why a society built upon such a principle will do better than others:

- A society made up of cooperative, socially-conscious individuals will be more a society of progress and achievement than one that isn't - and will be happier in the bargain;

- Cooperative society is more fulfilling to human nature, which is inherently gregarious; people are social beings, and our social separations are artificial, not natural; people tend to experience their deepest joys with others, not in solitude;

- Allegiance to the greater good inspires individuals to reach beyond themselves, to pursue wider interests; such efforts, driven by loyalty to one's family and neighbors, imparts stability and harmony, as well as cultivating empathy and a genuine feeling of happiness in the accomplishments of others.

Lamont presents a strong case, and most humanists would affirm both his reasoning and his sentiment. And we can also feel echoes of his argument in our observations of *Trek* culture, and the values we observe within Starfleet in particular.

Do We Naturally Seek the Greater Good?

Lamont argues above that the greater good isn't just preferable, it's innate – built into human beings. Is he right?

In his book *Why We Cooperate*, developmental psychologist Michael Tomasello addresses the following question: is cooperation between human beings a naturally emergent behavior or a learned one?

Either way, it's great that it exists, but the implications for our thesis – that human beings possess the inherent goodness in which Gene Roddenberry believed – are profound: if the former, then we have within us what we need to achieve a fully humanist future; if the latter, then it will be a far greater struggle, getting where we want to be.

Tomasello begins by pointing to research[50] demonstrating that infants as young as 18 months overwhelmingly attempt to assist adults whose hands are full. He cites this as one of five reasons to believe that this cooperative impulse in very small children is a naturally emergent human trait. It's the first of five:

1. Very small children impulsively help others without prompting or training;
2. Parental reward does not alter the outcome of #1; the child will impulsively help with or without reward;
3. Chimpanzee infants exhibit the same behaviors;
4. Human children exhibit the behavior across a diverse range of cultures;
5. Experiments have shown that helping behavior in young children is mediated by empathy – they will tend to help an adult they perceive to be a victim before helping another.

Tomasello continues to methodically develop a portrait of cooperation as evolutionary, building toward this conclusion: "...the changes we see in human societies beginning with the advent of agriculture and cities are not due, on anyone's account, to any kind of biological adaptation," he wrote. "The changes would seem to be sociological only, given their recency and the fact that by this time modern humans were already spread out all over the glove (so that a species-wide biological change was highly unlikely). What this means is that most, if not all, of the highly complex forms of cooperation in modern industrial societies – from the United Nations to credit card purchases over the Internet – are built primarily on cooperative skills ant motivations biologically evolved for

---

[50] *Not by Genes Alone: How Culture Transformed Human Evolution*, Peter Richardson and Robert Boyd. University of Chicago Press, 2006.

---

small-group interactions: the kinds of altruistic and collaborative activities that we have seen here in our simple studies of great apes and young children."

We have good reason to believe, then, that the deep cooperation that binds not just humanity but all the worlds of the Federation in Roddenberry's 23rd century doesn't need to be contrived; it just needs to be awakened.

Lost in Space

Genetic variety in both our ancient (limbic) and modern (cortical) brain components – those contributing to social reasoning, in particular – gives us a group of distinct cognitive "types," each with different cognitive strengths and decision-making style. No one human mind can encompass the variety expressed by this range of distinct types; it takes a group of humans – a diverse group, with many persons of each type – fully express the potential of human reason and decision-making. And that potential, by evolution's hand, is how humankind has managed to meet the needs of the many, since our beginnings.

The problem is... we've lost our way. Our modern social organization robs of us the value of the cognitive diversity that we absolutely will need to meet the challenges that threaten us, both today and tomorrow.

Exceptions to the Rule

In 2246, the governor of the Tarsus IV colony – a man named Kodos – is faced with the starvation of the 8,000 Federation colonists under his governance when a fungus destroys the food supply. In a terrifying totalitarian gesture, he orders half the colonists killed so that the remainder might survive on what little food remained until relief arrives. He himself decides who would live and who would die.[51]

"The revolution is successful," he declared to the colonists, "but survival depends upon drastic measures. Your continued existence represents a threat to the well-being of society. Your lives mean slow death to the more valued members of the colony. Therefore, I have no alternative but to sentence you to death. Your execution is so ordered."

A dozen years later, Pike's *Enterprise* intercepts and rescues an alien shuttle harboring a young boy, fleeing a non-Federation planet where he is presumably to be honored with the status of First Servant of his people. Pike and company are convinced by those pursuing the boy that he was being kidnapped, and that they are doing a good thing by returning him. Later, they learn that the boy's "Ascension" to the position of First Servant involves a ceremony where he is plugged into a vast machine, for life. This machine controls their society – and, in particular, it keeps their cities floating in the clouds, far above the unfriendly surface of the planet, which everyone very much enjoys.[52]

Pike is horrified to learn that he has aided and abetted in bringing about this boy's monstrous fate. He confronts the woman who has been explaining it all to him.

"What did you do to that boy?" Pike demands.
"The Ascension is complete," she says, "You may go."

---

[51] In "The Conscience of the King", *Star Trek: The Original Series* (S1E13)

[52] In "Lift Us Where Suffering Cannot Reach", *Star Trek: Strange New Worlds* (S1/E6)

"You're damn right I'm going," Pike answers, "getting that child the hell away from that thing."

"Even if you could get into the Chamber, severing the connection would only kill him."

"Why?"

"Serving Majalis is his destiny. His reason for being."

"You plugged a kid into a machine. What's it gonna do to him?"

"We don't know," she replies. "The machine needs the neural network of a child to function. Our founders designed it that way. We don't know why. We've hunted for centuries for alternatives and found nothing. It was the purpose of my research when we met."

"Will he suffer?"

"Yes. We don't pretend otherwise. We live in gratitude for him. And when a new First Servant ascends, we will live for her."

"Your whole civilization," Pike rails in disgust, "all your – this. It's all founded on the suffering of a child... The first chance I get, I'm reporting this to Starfleet."

Both of these *Trek* scenarios fall into the same category as those mentioned at the top of the chapter: an individual or individuals must sacrifice greatly for the benefit of the many. But while we found nobility in the first scenarios, there's something morally onerous in these latter ones. We can ask, then – is the greater good always a higher priority than the individual?

We can begin by noting that in the story of Kodos the Executioner, we have a single person implementing his own version of the greater good by force, without the consent of those over whom he has authority. He acts unilaterally and mercilessly. And, in the end, in vain; relief ships arrived ahead of schedule, rendering the execution of the colonists nothing more than an unnecessary slaughter.

The humanist would rightly argue that the deliberation Kodos undertook to select his course of action was distinctly *non*-humanist: it was purely authoritarian, rather than cooperative; the sacrifices that occurred were involuntary, and that, too, is distinctly non-humanist. Moreover, he implemented his own misguided notions of eugenics, in deciding who was worthy of survival and who wasn't; a humanist would not make such distinctions, embracing instead the principle that all of the colonists were equally worthy.

As for Pike and Majalis and the boy who was plugged into his planet, the argument can be made that the boy accepted his fate voluntarily. He was terrified, but he *chose* to become First Servant. The counter-argument, of course, is that no child should ever be faced with such a horrifying choice, but we can go further still: the solution of plugging a small child into a machine that runs the planet is one of convenience, not survival. The surface of Majalis is described as very inhospitable, and its citizens live in floating cities that are really comfortable; surrendering their current lifestyle and returning to live on their planet's surface, which their technology could clearly facilitate, would be supremely *un*-comfortable.

Imposing suffering on a minority to preserve the comfort of a majority is not a choice a humanist society would make. Moreover, the effort required to bring about a society that could embrace the principle the Majalans have set aside is exactly the kind of undertaking that defines humanism: working together to enable a better way of living for all. If that means coming down out of the clouds and taking the hard work of re-taming a world, so be it. The society that makes that very humanist choice is the stronger one.

The greater good – the needs of the many – is clearly the guiding light of the Roddenberry future, as visualized by *Star*

Trek. A galaxy where poverty and oppression have been vanquished, where everyone enjoys sustenance and dignity and opportunity, can only happen when the greater good is the social priority, above wealth and power and status. It's that vision, a future defined by a moral clarity and ethical maturity far beyond what we've achieved so far, that draws many to the *Trek* mythos: they want to live in the Roddenberry future.

And that's the future a successful resistance can bring.

"May we together become greater than the sum of both of us."

Infinite Diversity
in Infinite Combinations

"Alexander, where I come from, size, shape, or color makes no difference."

~Kirk

Few attributes of the *Star Trek* universe stand out as starkly as its commitment to the concept of diversity. From the debut of the original series, the broadcast of the very first episode on Sept. 8, 1966, audiences could see that commitment up close. Alongside the white guy stood an Asian, a black woman, a Southerner, an alien – and, before long, a Russian.

That commitment would continue through series after series, as *Trek* gave us a multiracial family (Chief O'Brien and Keiko on *Deep Space Nine*), a black captain (Sisko), a female captain (Janeway) – and, here in the 21st century, a black female starship captain (Michael Burnham on *Discovery*), a number of LGBTQ characters in her crew; *Voyager*'s Seven of Nine in a same-sex relationship on *Star Trek: Picard*; Spock and Uhura in a relationship in the Kelvin Timeline, as well as Sulu's family.

That diversity was nestled not only in the core of *Trek*, but in Gene Roddenberry's own humanism. He commented on it many times, summing it up as follows:

> "If man is to survive, he will have learned to take a delight in the essential differences between men and between cultures. He will learn that differences in ideas and attitudes are a delight, part of life's exciting variety, not something to fear."

Trek's diversity commentary extended beyond race and sexuality to mind, spirit, and life in any form. From Spock's reconciliation of his own dual nature to Sisko's participation in the Bajoran faith, from Janeway's acceptance of ex-Borg Seven of Nine to the friendship between Geordi LaForge and Data, *Trek* has celebrated diversity endlessly, living up to its creators' humanist vision.

Kirk himself expressed it perfectly in "The Savage Curtain": "We've each learned to be delighted with what we are." That self-acceptance – the social norm in *Trek*'s idealized human future – reflects a universal acceptance and tolerance that pervades humanity through the 23rd century and beyond.

We might even note the very stark contrast between that beautiful social norm and the much darker one that permeates the Federation's most horrifying adversary, the Borg – a vast collective of beings completely stripped of all individuality. Anti-diversity.

We can even note that diversity is so deeply inculcated in *Trek* that we notice it most when it goes missing:

The Horta has killed 50 miners on Janus VI and placed the lives of everyone in the colony at risk – and the surviving miners want it dead. But Spock discovers that the Horta is no monster, but a mother protecting her young: the miners have been destroying the useless silicon nodules they keep finding, which are in fact her eggs. When they threaten to attack the creature, Kirk levels his phaser at them: "The first man that fires is dead!" The dedication to diversity here is clear, not only in the defense of the Horta by Kirk and Spock, but by the ready acceptance of the miners, once the situation is made clear to them.[53]

Alexander has been stripped of his dignity, reduced to slavery and literally treated like a house pet by his fellow Platonian colonists, all of whom have become incorrigible narcissists since acquiring telekinetic powers - which Alexander lacks, leaving him at their mercy. Alexander is a dwarf, and is mocked and demeaned for it.[54]

Kirk befriends him, and seeks to learn from him about the power of the other colonists:

"Alexander, are there other Platonians like you?"

"What do you mean, 'like me?'" Alexander asked guardedly.

"Who don't have the psychokinetic ability," Kirk clarifies.

Alexander is relieved. "I thought you were talking about my size, because they make fun of me for my size. But, to answer your question, I'm the only one without it. I was brought here as the court buffoon. That's why I'm everybody's slave and I have to be ten places at once, and I

---

[53] In "The Devil in the Dark", *Star Trek: The Original Series* (S1/E25)

[54] In "Plato's Stepchildren", *Star Trek: The Original Series* (S3/E10)

never do anything right."

Spock asks Alexander about the power, and Kirk comments that he and the other *Enterprise* officers are perfectly happy without it.

"You know, I believe you are," Alexander responds. "Listen, where you come from, are there a lot of people without the power, and my size?"

"Alexander, where I come from, size, shape, or color makes no difference."

These examples (and there are, of course, many more) project an image of a society that has embraced diversity in all its forms, just as Roddenberry foresaw. The citizens of the Federation and the personnel of Starfleet in particular have gotten over the racism, ethnocentrism, misogyny and other social toxins that still contaminate humankind today.

It is exactly this commitment to diversity, and the recognition that its absence is toxic to us all, that motivates humanists. It is an integral part of the humanist social framework, and tops the list of humanist aspirations for our progress as a species.

Otherness vs. Sameness

The health and benefit of diversity might seem so obvious and essential that it might baffle those who embrace it that anyone would feel otherwise. But, of course, many do; on the flip side of diversity we find xenophobia – more recently rebranded *othering*, the ancient tradition of lumping some people into a rejected or despised group apart from one's own.

Othering serves up mirror-image versions of diversity's categories: there is ethnic othering, religious othering, gender- or sex-based othering. Political othering, in particular, has made a spectacle of itself in recent years.

What is at the core of othering?

"Othering is not about liking or disliking someone," wrote John A. Powell in *The Guardian*. "It is based on the conscious or unconscious assumption that a certain identified group poses a threat to the favoured group. It is largely driven by politicians and the media, as opposed to personal contact. Overwhelmingly, people don't "know" those that they are Othering."

It's that threat that drives otherness, wrote Čega se bojiš on Wordpress. "The fear of otherness is closely linked to the fear of the unknown and to the degree of trust in people. It is based on the fact that someone by their existence endangers what we consider 'our own' or 'ours.' It is often manifested in the form of fear that someone who has a different cultural characteristic to us – such as faith, language, customs and value system – endangers 'our' culture and way of life. According to this matrix, the influx of other people's elements into our cultural register leads to the long-term loss of 'our' identity and cultural affiliation.

"Otherness does not often come from far away. It is found in the neighbourhood, partly in the society and community to which we belong. Someone from a rival fan camp, someone on an opposing political-ideological spectrum, someone of extremely different material possibilities or understanding of sexual orientation and gender affiliation is a representative of the otherness which in the most radical forms often becomes a source of collective and individual fears."

In a 2016 interview by Jeffrey Goldberg in *The Atlantic*, then-President Barack Obama cited othering as the primary source of most of the world's conflict: "tribe - us/them, a hostility toward the unfamiliar or unknown." It's not hard to see this reality reflected in even a cursory reading of human history; anywhere diversity has been lacking, othering has flourished, to the detriment at all.

Humanists, whose focus is persistently fixed on a positive

human future, understandably see othering as a significant barrier to be addressed in progressing toward that future. The embrace and tireless nourishing of diversity everywhere is essential to tearing down that barrier.

Roddenberry's IDIC

In the third season of the original series, the story is famously told that Roddenberry, who had spun up a side business selling *Trek* memorabilia, created a Vulcan medallion, to be worn on a necklace – the "IDIC", which stands for "Infinite Diversity in Infinite Combinations". Leonard Nimoy was to wear the medallion in an upcoming episode, "Is There in Truth No Beauty?" The idea was to create a new *Trek* artifact that he could sell through the mail, and putting it in an episode was basically free advertising.

Nimoy and Shatner both objected. This was blatant opportunism, Roddenberry exploiting the show for personal gain.

Nimoy: "Certainly, I was all in favor of the philosophy behind the IDIC," he wrote in his memoir *I Am Spock*, "but not the fact that Gene wanted me to wear the medallion because he wanted to sell them through his mail-order business, Lincoln Enterprises. Where the scene had been problematic creatively for me, it now was problematic ethically.

"Although I didn't appreciate Spock being turned into a billboard, I at least felt that the IDIC idea had more value than the content of the original scene."

Shatner, in his *Star Trek Memories*: "I called [producer] Fred [Freiberger] down to the set, asking him, 'What this "IDIC" thing all about?' I knew that Lincoln Enterprises would soon be selling these things, and there was no way I was going to muck up a perfectly good story line just so we could include Gene's rather thinly veiled commercial."

The scene was rewritten, with the explanation of the idea

behind the medallion now being Nimoy's job. Since that idea appealed to him, even if the scene itself did not, he gracefully compromised – and now we have the IDIC concept to celebrate as a core principle of *Trek*, memorabilia marketing aside.

Was Roddenberry being opportunistic? Yes. He himself, to his credit, didn't even try to pretend otherwise. But does the conflict diminish in any way *Trek*'s obvious, pervasive and consistent embrace of IDIC? Not at all.

In fact, Roddenberry went out of his way to tie our potential to achieve the future he foretold very firmly to the embrace of diversity.

> "*Star Trek* was an attempt to say humanity will reach
> maturity and wisdom on the day that it begins not just
> to tolerate but take a special delight in differences in
> ideas and differences in lifeforms."

Our successful transition to the stars, he argued tirelessly, is inevitably dependent upon our achieving exactly the embrace of diversity that the IDIC celebrates:

> "Diversity contains as many treasures as those waiting
> for us on other worlds," he said. "We will find it
> impossible to fear diversity and to enter the future at
> the same time."

And this:

> "If we cannot learn to actually enjoy those small
> differences, to take a positive delight in those small
> differences between our own kind, here on this planet,
> then we do not deserve to go out into space and meet

the diversity that is almost certainly out there."

Diversity and Inclusion, *Trek*-style

The diversity of *Trek* changed both television and science fiction, as Roddenberry's advocacy of humanism brought it to the fore. Maintaining that commitment through more than five decades, a dozen spin-off series and 13 feature films, it has adapted to the times, manifesting differently in each.

"Inclusiveness has always been at the core of *Star Trek*," wrote Swapna Krisha on www.superculture.com. "And in fulfilling Roddenberry's vision, each series of the show has been quietly revolutionary. It's fundamental to what *Star Trek* is as a franchise.

"But in the 1960s, diversity meant something very different than what it does today. And that's what is so incredible about this franchise, and why it's currently experiencing another cultural renaissance: It's dynamic. It's always been an allegory, helping us grapple with our imperfect world by showing us a kind of utopia that we can strive for. *Star Trek* has always shown us what we are capable of - a vision of a better, kinder future. And as the years pass, it changes and reinvents itself to stay relevant."

This constant renewal of its diversity theme has kept *Trek* in a position of leadership among its peers, while positioning it as a touchstone for the humanism it so capably models.

"The amount of positive representation *Discovery* and *Star Trek*'s other new shows have included has put the franchise far out in front of any other modern sci-fi in terms of diversity," wrote Dana Hanson of Screenrant. "When compared to movie franchises like *Star Wars* or the Marvel Cinematic Universe, *Star Trek* shows them both up time and again."

And accusations that the ethnic diversity of the original series amounted to hollow tokenism have fallen away from the franchise as a whole.

"Besides pushing cultural boundaries, *Star Trek* has portrayed people of color not as tokens, but as complex characters with relationships," wrote Nancy Wang Yuen on HuffPost. "The father-son relationship of Benjamin and Jake Sisko (*Star Trek: Deep Space Nine*) and Keiko O'Brien's interracial family (*Star Trek: The Next Generation* and *Star Trek: Deep Space Nine*) are seldom portrayed on television."

The presentation of diversity on the bridge of the original *Enterprise* did more than break social and cultural ground; it brought to the forefront the dreams of many that humanity pursue that future literally.

"For all the positives and problems within the original series -- reflecting as they do the wider positives and problems of the liberal American left - *Star Trek*'s conflicting representations of race, gender and politics nonetheless stuck in cultural memory," wrote Katrina Ojaste in "Infinite Diversity in Infinite Combinations: *Star Trek*, the Sixties & the American Left". "Characters such as Uhura, Sulu and Chekov are remembered not as somewhat problematic representations of an idealized future but as real, ground-breaking figures of early television. Roddenberry's future, though imperfect, became the vision that others wanted to see come true. Much of today's television criticism relies on issues of representation, and any show that dares present an image of the future that does not reflect the realities and diversities of today is not destined for long-term success. This does not necessarily mean that the *Star Trek* of the sixties no longer reflects the future we want to see: of all the many series in the franchise, it was the original 1960s one that has been revived recently."

Nichelle Nichols, who earned the endorsement of Martin Luther King, Jr. with her portrayal of the black, female communications officer Nyota Uhura on the original series, went on in the Seventies to become a spokesperson for NASA, recruiting women and minority members into the space program. Among those she brought in were Sally Ride, the first American female astronaut; Col Guion Bluford, the first black astronaut; Judith Resnik and Ron McNair. Astronaut Mae Jemison, who is both female and black, not only cited Nichols as her inspiration, but poignantly went on to appear on *Star Trek: The Next Generation*.

This very active, very humanist pursuit of diversity was remembered and celebrated by NASA in 2021, when it observed Gene Roddenberry's 100th birthday with a special event, "Celebrating Gene Roddenberry: Star Trek's Bridge and NASA". Gene's son Rod, now an executive producer in the new *Star Trek* franchise, was a featured panelist.

In an interview with *Variety*, the younger Roddenberry reiterated *Trek*'s humanist commitment.

"If we all do the same thing every day, we don't grow, we don't evolve, we don't learn anything. And so it is the diversity in everything, whether it's something outside, different trees, different looking people. But more importantly, it's the difference in idea. The Enterprise and the crew weren't out exploring the galaxy, looking just for weird looking aliens. They were for species that looked at the universe in a different way than we did.

"Because up to that point, humanity had finally come together and realized that it's our diversity that makes us special. We realized working together, we can do so much more. And so now we were trying to find people who looked at the universe in a different way, because we knew that we could grow and evolve by hearing something we'd never heard before. And whether we agreed with it or not, it was the hearing of that, the analyzing of it and the taking pieces out of it that we agreed with and incorporating into our own that allowed us to grow."

Before Kirk, Spock and Uhura stands a being in the image

of Abraham Lincoln, a personal hero of Kirk's. In the course of their exchange, 'Lincoln' fears he has offended Uhura – by calling her a 'charming Negress'.[55]

"But why should I object to that term, sir?" Uhura asks. "You see, in our century, we've learned not to fear words."

"The foolishness of my century had me apologizing where no offense was given," Lincoln replies.

Kirk sums it up: "We've each learned to take delight in what we are. The Vulcans learned that centuries before we did."

Infinite Diversity, in Infinite Combinations - IDIC. It is a guiding principle of Vulcan philosophy, the center of their value system. *Kol-Ut-Shan*[56] in the native tongue, it celebrates differences in-kind and beyond, and is part of their historical path to universal peace.

We first saw the IDIC – a medallion reflecting the concept – in the episode "Is There in Truth No Beauty?", hanging around Spock's neck at a dinner honoring Dr. Miranda Jones, a human telepath preparing to mind-meld with a very non-human Medusan. Spock connects the medallion to the philosophy: "The triangle and the circle - different shapes, materials, textures - represent any two diverse things which come together to create here, truth or beauty."

Though Gene Roddenberry created the medallion so he'd have a new toy to sell to fans, the philosophy of IDIC was a winner with the cast, the crew, and everyone in the *Star Trek* universe. It perfectly embodies the humanist theme of the show.

"Infinite Diversity in Infinite Combinations represents a

---

[55] In "The Savage Curtain", *Star Trek: The Original Series* (S3/E22)

[56] From "Gravity," *Star Trek: Voyager.*

Vulcan belief that beauty, growth, progress, all result from the union of the unlike. Concord, as much as discord, requires the presence of at least two different notes," Roddenberry explained. "The brotherhood of man is an ideal based on learning to delight in our essential differences, as well as learning to recognize our similarities. The circle and triangle combine to produce the gemstone in the center as the union of words and music creates song, or the union of marriage creates children."[57]

And it can honestly be said that Roddenberry's attitude toward diversity was present from the start, evident in his eventual casting of the show, with its multinational crew. It's a statement that is apparent to any viewer in their first few moments of watching any
episode, a statement that persisted through all of *Trek*'s on-screen incarnations.

But it's about more than variety in skin color and culture: diversity lurks deep beneath our surface – and is perhaps more survival-critical than any other aspect of humanism.

The Ancient Human IDIC

But diversity is more than a key to future harmony and growth. Diversity was, ironically, the key to human survival, when we were genetically at our most Homogenous.

Confined in our earlier millennia to Central Africa, we had not yet developed the broad range of skin tones we now enjoy; our culture in particular was decidedly monotone, as we had not yet developed writing, art, or even language.

Yet we had already begun experiencing the most important diversity of all: differences in thought.

By this, we aren't thinking of differences in philosophies or

---

doctrines or ideologies like those that surround us today – those things didn't yet exist. We're talking about *literal* differences in thought – the actual variations that existed (and still exist!) in human brains, diversity in proportional quantities of brain tissue in different brain regions – diversity that resulted (and still does today) in some variation in how each of us processes the world.

We've looked at those brain variations themselves, and how different combinations of brain components resulted in different cognitive contributions to tribal survival. And we've considered how destructive it is when that cognitive diversity is dampened when humans cluster together in cults of like-mindedness. Now let's look at the evidence.

Diversity Makes Us Smarter

"Great things in business are never done by one person. They're done by a team of people."

~Steve Jobs

Scientific American gathered together summaries of a number of studies demonstrating the advantages of diversity in the workplace,[58] concluding that being around people who think differently increases our creativity and diligence.

Cristian Deszö of the University of Maryland and David Ross of Columbia University, for instance, noted the impact of gender diversity in business. Reviewing the size and gender make-up of the top equity firms from 1992-2006, they found that, on average, firms with women in top management positions demonstrated greater financial performance than those without. Orlando Richard of the University of Texas found in a 2003 study that the same holds true for racial

---

[58] In *Scientific American*, Oct. 2014.

diversity in upper management.

A 2006 study at the University of Illinois teamed subjects to solve a murder mystery exercise, varying the racial make-up of the three-person teams. Teams with a non-white member significantly out-performed all-white teams.

Another University of Illinois study in 2013 tasked subjects to identify as either Democrat or Republican, then read a murder mystery and decide who they thought committed the crime.

They were then tasked to write an essay making their case, for presentation to another test subject in hopes of convincing them. Half of the subjects were told they would be making the case to a member of their own political party; half were told they'd be trying to convince a member of the other party. Subjects of both parties prepared less well and wrote a less persuasive essay when they believed they were going to be talking to a member of their own party. "Diversity jolts us into cognitive action in ways that Homogeneity simply does not," the study concluded.

And in 2014, Richard Freeman and Wei Huang of Harvard University examined ethnicity among the authors of 1.5 million scientific papers, noting that those written by ethnically diverse research teams received more citations than those written by teams of people with common ethnicity.

Finally there's a 2006 study by Samuel Sommers of Tufts University, where real judges, jury administrators and jurors participated in a mock jury experiment to determine the effects of racial diversity in jury decision-making. Sommers arranged the jurors into all-white groups and four-white, two-black groups. The diverse juries made fewer errors in recall of important information and discussed the role of race in the case more openly. Sommers concluded that in the presence of diversity, white jurors "were more diligent and open-minded," according to *Scientific American*.

Cognitive diversity and performance

But gender, race, and political orientation, though qualifying as diversity, do not necessarily imply *cognitive* diversity. In an article in the *Harvard Business Review,*[59] Alison Reynolds and David Lewis took up the problem, using Peter Robertson's AEM
Cube[60] tool to assess a person's knowledge processing and perspective in new situations.

Six teams were created, variable in their degree of AEM Cube ratings, and were then given a group task to complete. The teams with greater diversity in knowledge processing and perspective completed the exercise more quickly; the greater the level of diversity, the higher the team's score.

Reynolds and Lewis further noted that cognitive diversity is a more reliable performance enhancer than gender and racial diversity, comparing the AEM Cube study to other performance studies:

"Someone being from a different culture or a different generation gives no clue as to how that person might process information, engage with, or respond to change," they wrote. "We cannot easily detect cognitive diversity from the outside. It cannot be predicted or easily orchestrated. The very fact that

---

[59] "Teams Solve Problems Faster When They're Cognitively Diverse," March 30, 2017

[60] The AEM Cube is an assessment tool that measures three axes of personality: Attachment, Exploration, and Managing contribution (approach to complexity). It is called a "cube" because the results can be mapped to three-dimensional space.

it is an internal difference requires us to work hard to surface it and harness the benefits."

Cognitive diversity aboard the *Enterprise*

Though Roddenberry may not have been thinking of it at the time, the bridge of the *Enterprise* gives us yet another example of the merits of cognitive diversity: it is difficult to imagine two people whose information processing styles differ more than Spock and McCoy, and the stylistic disparity is greater still when the rest of the bridge officers are added to the mix. Yet the integration of these differences is what informs Kirk's decisions and viewpoint, time and again.

Vonda McIntyre's *Trek* novel *Enterprise: The First Adventure* (1987) takes an interesting turn here: when Kirk is first given command, the admiral giving it to him rejects his choice of his best friend, Gary Mitchell, as first officer, insisting that Spock, who has served on the ship for years under Captain Christopher Pike, be promoted into the role. The admiral's argument is that Kirk and Mitchell are too much alike, and that both Kirk and the crew will benefit from a command team with greater differences.

Finally, we have the words of Surak, the father of Vulcan philosophy, spoken to Kirk later in "The Savage Curtain":

> "In my time, we knew not of Earthmen. I
> am pleased to see that we have differences.
> May we together become greater than the
> sum of both of us."

"All members of the Federation have a voice in its governance."

The Essence of Democracy:
We Listen to Each Other

The R'ongovians are a non-aligned alien people whose territory lies between Klingon and Romulan space, along Starfleet's route into the Beta Quadrant. Starfleet has dispatched Pike's *Enterprise* to engage in a dialog with them. A young Lt. Spock is present as Pike speaks with their leaders.[61]

"You are Vulcan?" One of the R'ongovians asks Spock. "Famous for your logic, yes?"

"Indeed," Spock replies.

"Then, your voice is also part of the Federation?"

"All members of the Federation have a voice in its governance," Spock explains.

"That sounds... confusing."

This draws a chuckle from Pike. "Yeah, it can be."

"With so many voices in your Federation, how do you

---

[61] In "Spock Amok", *Star Trek: Strange New Worlds* (S1/E5)

decide which one is in control?"

Pike gets serious.

"We vote," he declares. "We gain our power from all our membership, so we try to listen to each other. All of us."

We first became acquainted with the power of Federation democracy in "Journey to Babel" in the original series, when Kirk's *Enterprise* trucked more than 100 Federation delegates to a neutral planetoid to discuss and vote on the admission of Coridan to its ranks. We saw argument, contentiousness – and a serious, violent effort to disrupt the democratic process and usurp its outcome.

The actual story of human democracy – egalitarian self-governance within a social group – is more complex than we generally learn while growing up, and at the same time more universal than we've been led to believe.

It's more complex in that the great American Experiment that commenced in the 18th century is often portrayed as a reflection of the Roman Republic, in form, and a product of the French Enlightenment, in philosophy. The form – representative government of all citizens – was a loose match, but fair enough; the philosophy – that human beings, living in a democratic order, are at their natural best – was a much stronger match, heavily derivative of the work of John Locke and Jean-Jacques Rousseau.

The thing is – though many of us were brought up with this basic understanding of where modern democracy originated, Roman Republic to the French Enlightenment to America's Framers – that's just the bare bones of the actual story.

From Rome to Britain to France

Thom Hartmann provides a deeper take in his book *The Hidden History of American Democracy*. Yes, he writes, Ben

Franklin and John Adams and Thomas Jefferson all went to Europe and picked up a lot of Enlightenment thought – and, yes, they were well versed in the political philosophy of the Roman Republic – but where did the French philosophers get *their* inspiration?

It turns out that inspiration came full circle: they got it from *the social order of the Native Americans.*

Hartmann notes that the thinkers of the Enlightenment were at first replying, in no small measure, to the 17th century writings of Thomas Hobbes, a British philosopher who posited that the natural human was a brutish, savage creature, only tamed through the use of political and social force. In his book *Leviathan*, Hobbes took the stance that only a powerful autocratic state or rigidly enforced religion was capable of bringing order to humankind; without it, anarchy would inevitably prevail. After all, wasn't such a structure to be seen in all nation-states, back to the beginning of civilization? Aren't *all* societies ruled by powerful, wealthy kings or rigid priesthoods?

Over the next century, a new generation of philosophers recoiled from that ghastly vision. Hobbes's countryman John Locke, in his *Two Treatises of Government* and *An Essay Concerning Human Understanding*, argued that the former's cynical take on human nature, however biblical it might be, was far off the mark; human beings, Locke suggested, are *not* born evil, are *not* naturally violent and selfish, and do *not* require dominant men of power and wealth to create a successful social order.

Locke had a millennium of European history working against him, but was undeterred; the truth of human nature was true irrespective of how long it had been apparent, he argued. He proceeded, in the face of much criticism, to suggest that "Man being born, as has been proved, with a title to perfect freedom and an uncontrolled enjoyment of all the rights and privileges of the law of nature, equally with any other man, or number of men in the world, hath by nature a power, not only to preserve his property, that is, life, liberty, and estate, against the injuries and attempts of other men."

He went on to write that "Nature, I confess, has put into man a desire of happiness and an aversion to misery: these indeed are innate practical principles."

These two statements, Hartmann points out, were synthesized by Thomas Jefferson in the Declaration of Independence.

Later came Jean-Jacques Rousseau, who connected the benign natural state of humanity advanced by Locke into a political form, suggesting (per Hartmann) that "the laws of nature were essentially democratic and noble and that the closer humanity could come to following natural law, the closer we'd be to a life of freedom and happiness."

Hartmann goes on to quote Rousseau: "There you see how luxury, dissolution, and slavery have in every age been the punishment for the arrogant efforts we have made in order to emerge from the happy ignorance where Eternal Wisdom had placed us."

Rousseau was adding the touch that wealth, power and social dominance didn't seem to have a place in Nature's Eternal Wisdom or Happy Ignorance. This, the Framers synthesized with Locke's assertion that while "divine law" placed men in authority over other men, Nature's law was based on their approval of their governors: a government was only legitimate if it derived that legitimacy from the "consent of the governed."

That's a powerful idea, and if we left it at that, we'd still have a narrative that was coherent and functional. But there are, Hartmann says, two additional layers.

Beyond the Human Being

Suppose Locke was right, and Nature's laws favored democratic community? Wouldn't this necessarily extend beyond humankind? After all, there are other social animals on the planet.

Hartmann points out that science has, in recent years, confirmed that this is indeed the case:[62]

"In the first paragraph of the Declaration of Independence, Jefferson wrote that 'the laws of nature and of nature's God' compelled America's Founders to reject British oligarchy and embrace democracy," Hartmann wrote. "But was he right? Is nature actually democratic? Biologists Tim Roper and L. Conradt at the School of Life Sciences, University of Sussex, England, studied this issue in animals.

"'We've always assumed that the alpha or leader animal of the herd or group makes the decision, and the others follow, like the human kings and queens of old. The leader knows best, we believe: he or she is prepared for that genetically by generations of Darwinian natural selection.

"But it turns out there's a system for voting among animals, from honeybees to primates, that we've just never noticed because we weren't looking for it. 'Many authors have assumed despotism without testing [for democracy],' Conradt and Roper wrote in a *Nature* article about the study, 'because the feasibility of democracy, which requires the ability to vote and to count votes, is not immediately obvious in non-humans.' Stepping into this vacuum of knowledge, the two scientists decided to create a testable model that 'compares the synchronization costs of despotic and democratic groups.'

"Conradt and Roper discovered that when a single leader (what they call a despot) or a small group of leaders (the animal equivalent of an oligarchy) makes the choices, the swings into extremes of behavior tend to be greater and more dangerous to the long-term survival of the group. Because in a despotic model the overall needs of the entire group are measured only by the leader's needs, wrong decisions would be made often enough to put the survival of the group at risk. With

---

[62] In Hartmann's *The Hidden History of American Oligarchy*, pp. 52-54.

democratic decision-making, however, the overall knowledge and wisdom of the entire group, as well as the needs of the entire group, come into play. The outcome is less likely to harm anybody, and the group's probability of survival is enhanced. 'Democratic decisions are more beneficial primarily because they tend to produce less extreme decisions,' they noted in the abstract to their paper.

"Britain's leading mass-circulation science journal, *New Scientist*, looked at how Conradt and Roper's model played out in the natural world. They examined the behavior of a herd of red deer, which are social animals with alpha leaders. What they found was startling: Red deer always behave democratically. When more than half of the animals were pointing at a particular watering hole, for example, the entire group would then move in that direction. 'In the case of real red deer,' James Randerson noted, 'the animals do indeed vote with their feet by standing up. Likewise, with groups of African buffalo, individuals decide where to go by pointing in their preferred direction. The group takes the average and heads that way.' This explains in part the flock, swarm, and school nature of birds, gnats, and fish. With each wingbeat or fin motion, each member is 'voting' for the direction in which the flock, swarm, or school should move; when the 51 percent threshold is hit, the entire group moves as if telepathically synchronized.

"Tim Roper told me, 'Quite a lot of people have said, 'My gorillas do that,' or 'My animals do that.' On an informal, anecdotal basis, it [the article] seems to have triggered an 'Oh, yes, that's quite true' reaction in field workers.' I asked him if his theory that animals - and, by inference, humans in their 'natural state' - operate democratically contradicted Darwin. He was emphatic. 'I don't think it is [at variance with Darwin]... So the point about this model is that democratic decision-making is best for all the individuals in the group, as opposed to following a leader, a dominant individual. So we see it as an individual selection model, and so it's not incompatible with

Darwin at all.' Democracy, it turns out, is the norm in the animal kingdom, for the simple reason that it confers the greatest likelihood that the group will survive and prosper."

The Indigenous Critique

More than a few voices in paleontology and anthropology have suggested that Paleolithic humans were not at all savage and did not practice social dominance, but were instead egalitarian in their social order and equality-minded in their economics – owing, more than anything, to their lack of the concept of "property" or "wealth". What happened to one, happened to all; the members of any given human tribe were all in it together.

Civilization, originating in the Fertile Crescent and spreading throughout the Middle East in all directions, put an end to that. Agriculture, for all its power to feed more people and make possible the long-term storage of food – surplus – also bestowed the concepts of property and wealth, ownership, and stratified society. It was a very mixed blessing.

And when civilized humans began crossing the oceans and made their way to the Americas, they were closing that circle: humans who had lived through 200 generations of civilization, with its kings and armies and religions and treasures and poverty and slavery and genocides, found themselves face-to-face with humans who were *still in their Edenic state* – latter-day Paleoliths, still living according to Nature's laws, unsullied by wealth and property and class and autocracy.

Those humans included the Wendat, better known to history as the Huron tribe of the Iroquois Confederacy, encountered by French Jesuit missionaries who had hiked into Canada to save their souls. They were astonished by what they found.

"I do not believe there is any people on earth freer than they, and less able to allow the subjection of their wills to any power whatever," wrote Father Lallemant in *Jesuit Relations* in 1644, "so much so that Fathers here have no control over their children, or Captains over their subjects, or the Laws of the Country over any of them, except in so far as each is pleased to submit to them. There is no punishment which is inflicted on the guilty, and no criminal who is not sure that his life and property are in no danger."

How did the Wendat achieve this? "Consent of the governed" – the principle that would makes its way to Thomas Jefferson by way of Locke and Rousseau.

Governance among the Wendat was achieved Federation-style, as in the Babel conference over the Coridan question, as in the "we listen to each other" methodology that Captain Pike espouses to the R'ongovians.

"When the governed agreed, decisions were made or punishments meted out," Hartmann writes. "When they didn't, things were worked out in dialogue and debate, sometimes lasting days."

"This form of justice restrains all of these peoples, and seems more effectually to repress disorders than the personal punishment of criminals does in France," Lallemant wrote.

These writings took Europe by storm, triggering an insatiable curiosity about Native Americans that persisted for decades.

"I can say in truth that, as regards intelligence, they are in no wise inferior to Europeans and to those who dwell in France. I would never have believed that, without instruction, nature could have supplied a most ready and vigorous eloquence, which I have admired in many Hurons; or more clear-sightedness in public affairs, or a more discreet management in things to which they are accustomed."

The Baron De Lahontan, a Dutchman, would write, half a century later, of his dialogs with "an unusually brilliant Wendat statesman named Kandiaronk." His writings took up where the Jesuits had left off, giving Europe another look into the lives of humans still in Nature's arms, untouched by the afflictions of civilization. Ben Franklin was busy being born as those writings spread across Europe like wildfire, going through a dozen reprintings in a wide array of languages – and setting in motion the pens of the Enlightenment philosophers in Britain and France.

De Lahontan's dialog with his Wendat companion surfaced many criticisms of European society, overall a scathing indictment. Lahontan described Native America's own social order with astonishment:

"They think it unaccountable that one man should have more than another, and that the rich should have more respect than the poor. In short, they say, the name of 'savages', which we bestow upon them, would fit ourselves better, since there is nothing in our actions that bears an appearance of wisdom."

A 19-year-old Thomas Jefferson would meet such a Native American leader face to face – the Cherokee diplomat Ontasseté, who spent a great deal of time in colonial cities and towns, and would travel to England to negotiate a treaty with King George II. He and his brother Framers were very clear on the concepts by which these out-of-time people lived, how they managed their society. And it was on those ideas that they built the first true democracy in the civilized world.

It is easy, upon reflection, to see Federation society and governance as even more of a piece with Native America's way of living than with that of the United States. The latter is certainly less equalitarian than the other two, and the intrusion of wealth and power into the US political process unquestionably skews the Federation's concept of self-governance more toward that of the Iroquois Confederacy.

Which leaves us with a take-away: we face the rise of the authoritarian in the West today because we haven't gone far enough in the direction of either the Native America of the past or the Federation of the future. One of our *Trek*-inspired commitments must be, not only to the principle of governance by the consent of the governed, but the uncompromising practice of universal social and economic equality among the governed.

"This society must become united, or it will degenerate into total anarchy."

On the Other Side of Resistance

The humanoid inhabitants of Sigma Iotia are an imitative people, and a visit from the Federation Starship *Horizon* many decades earlier revved up that imitation: that ship's crew left a book behind, and the Iotians turned it into a holy book of sorts – they rebuilt their entire society around it.[63]

When Kirk's Enterprise visits Sigma Iotia, they find a world remade in the image of the Chicago of the 1920s – a world where criminal mobs rule, bosses are murderous authoritarians, all trying to take down the top boss, Bela Oymyx. Chaos reigns.

"One book on the gangs of Chicago did all this," McCoy comments. "It's amazing."

"They evidently seized upon that one book as the blueprint for an entire society," Spock replies.

"It's the Bible," McCoy adds.

"In old Chicago, conventional government almost broke down," Kirk says. "The gangs nearly took over."

"Yeah, well, Oxmyx is the worst gangster of all," McCoy notes.

---

[63] In "A Piece of the Action", *Star Trek: The Original Series* (S2/E17)

"We may quarrel with Mister Oxmyx' methods, but his goal is essentially the correct one," Spock points out. "This society must become united or it will degenerate into total anarchy."

Kirk and Spock are in the mess hall of a street mission in 1930 New York City, tasked with setting right the Federation timeline, which a deranged McCoy has accidentally disrupted. On the platform in the front of the room stands social worker Edith Keeler, who runs the mission. A visionary, she offers words of hope to the downtrodden men before her, peering boldly into the human future – the Federation future.

"Now I don't pretend to tell you how to find happiness and love when every day is just a struggle to survive," she says, "but I do insist that you *do* survive - because the days and the years ahead are worth living for! One day soon, man is going to be able to harness incredible energies, maybe even the atom. Energies that could ultimately hurl us to other worlds in some sort of spaceship. And the men that reach out into space will be able to find ways to feed the hungry millions of the world and to cure their diseases. They will be able to find a way to give each man hope and a common future, and those are the days worth living for! Our deserts will bloom!

"Prepare for tomorrow. Get ready. Don't give up!"[64]

The future of Edith Keeler's Depression-ridden New York City would be United Earth, as it's often referred to in *Trek*, centuries hence. There would come a day when no one on Earth, anywhere, would have to wait in life for a bowl of soup to survive the day. Everyone would be provided for, and would

---

[64] In "The City on the Edge of Forever", *Star Trek: The Original Series* (S1/E28)

be free to pursue whatever life they chose. Many would choose to roam the stars.

That future – and our own, if Earth is ever united – is by definition a future in which authoritarianism has been vanquished.

For the nations of the planet to join together in common cause, each contributing to a united humanity, there would necessarily be an end to the racism and misogyny that still plague us today. For that union to be a voluntary one, there would necessarily be a prevalent freedom and personal liberty available to all; those nations embracing those values would not tolerate their absence elsewhere, if true unity was the priority.

And such an international community would necessarily be economically strong, as its members work not for their own advantage but for mutual accommodation. Poverty would finally vanish.

All of these values are, of course anti-authoritarian values – as Roddenberry foresaw.

And while religion would certainly still exist, and that existence would certainly be sanctioned as within the bounds of freedom of personal choice, it would no longer set the political course of nations, nor define their populations. There could be no united Earth otherwise, for Christianity and Islam cannot even unite internally, and are each dedicated to the overthrow of the other. Judaism is not so threatening, but is no prone to compromise, let alone adaptation.

United Earth is an egalitarian Earth. And as globalization finally takes hold in the human story, we face a decisive moment.

"Perhaps the most exciting fact of modern humanism is that its world is becoming genuinely global and that it is viscerally and ideologically prepared for that fact," wrote Howard Radest, senior fellow at the Institute for Humanist Studies, in Anthony Pinn's *What is Humanism and Why Does It Matter?* "Humanist universalism is matched for the first time in history by geopolitical and cultural realities."

Globalization, and the human interconnectedness of the Internet in particular, are nudging humanity in a humanist direction, according to Krysia Gayle Solon, a scholar of the Humanist Alliance Philippines International.

"As the world has grown closer to each other because of globalization, so too has humanity," she said. "Humans have grown more trusting of one another rather than praying to the divines for answers or material objects. Instead of placing their trust solely in divine entities, many humans now rely on the wonders of science and prioritize progress for the good of mankind. Humanity has grown to be there for one another not because it was through the will of the divines, but because we have learned to be more thoughtful of others.

"This is Humanism, the act of placing more importance on other human beings rather than the divines. It encourages the people to utilize technological advancements, scientific discoveries, and innovations to ensure a bright future for the succeeding generations to come."

Charles Taylor, in his book *A Secular Age*, posits the nova effect: "...an ever-widening variety of moral/spiritual options, across the span of the thinkable and perhaps even beyond." Tone Svetelj of Boston College advances the idea that Taylor's nova effect is itself unifying in the paper "Universal Humanism – A Globalization Context is the Classroom of Unheard Options... how to Become More Human":

"...the humanism that includes all people and nations – for this reason I call it a universal humanism – allows us to discover in a new perspective what is universally human by transcending our spatial and temporal frames.

"Universal humanism permits us who live in modern Western societies to be at the deepest level of our existence in touch with commonalities among other human agents from the present and past times, both in and outside of Western societies. This humanism commits us to respect all specific definitions of humanism (Greek, Roman, German, Italian, Romantic, Christian, Muslim, Buddhist, exclusive, inclusive, and similar) on the one side, and on the other, challenges us to transcend them all and integrate each one of them into something what would be even more meaningful."

The Welsh writer Mick Antoniw makes the argument that the solutions to the specific problems that globalization is tugging into high relief are all contained within humanism:

"We live in a world where it is predicted that by 2030 50% of the world's wealth will be in the hands of 1% of the population. Half the world flourishes whilst half the world starves.

"As inequality increases, societies become increasingly unstable, growing nationalisms set people against people, barriers are erected and the seeds of conflict are sown.

"Humanism as with ethical socialism is about the belief that the power to resolve all these problems lies in our hands, through our rational analysis, through the use of science for the benefit of all through a recognition or our common humanity and obligations to one another."

Mike Whitty, a scholar for Global Citizens for Tolerance and Decency, sees globalization in its current state as fanning culture wars both within and between nations. He proposes humanism as a solution to that problem:

"Global humanism is an antidote to human alienation and fear thus the importance of outreach organizing to re-balance future evolution toward a future of tolerance and acceptance of our unity in diversity.

"Tolerance, civility and non-violence are the first steps toward a truce in the cultural wars. This truce buys time and allows freedom and liberty to grow in the hearts and minds of youth.

"Most thought leaders, especially tomorrow's youth, see the necessity of a live-and-let-live future, and acceptance of our circumstances until humanity evolves to a new paradigm of global humanism."

And, finally, the very reliable philosopher Bertrand Russell addresses the question of the future, putting a humanist spin on his most optimistic option, in his essay "The Future of Mankind":[65]

"Before the end of the present century, unless something quite unforeseeable occurs, one of three possibilities will have been realized. These three are:

- The end of human life, perhaps of all life on our planet.
- A reversion to barbarism after a catastrophic diminution of the population of the globe.
- A unification of the world under a single government, possessing a monopoly of all the major weapons of war.

"I do not pretend to know which of these will happen, or even which is the most likely. What I do contend is that the kind of system to which we have been accustomed cannot possibly continue.

- "The first possibility, the extinction of the human race, is not to be expected in the next world war, unless that war is postponed for a longer time than now seems probable. But if the next world war is indecisive, or if the victors are unwise, and if organized states survive it, a period of feverish technical development may be expected to follow its conclusion. With vastly more powerful means of utilizing atomic energy than those now available, it is thought by many sober men of science that

---

[65] Reprinted in his collection *Unpopular Essays*.

radioactive clouds, drifting round the world, may disintegrate living tissue everywhere. Although the last survivor may proclaim himself universal Emperor, his reign will be brief and his subjects will all be corpses. With his death the uneasy episode of life will end, and the peaceful rocks will revolve unchanged until the sun explodes.

- "The second possibility, that of a reversion to barbarism, would leave open the likelihood of a gradual return to civilization, as after the fall of Rome. The sudden transition will, if it occurs, be infinitely painful to those who experience it, and for some centuries afterwards life will be hard and drab. But at any rate there will still be a future for mankind, and the possibility of rational hope.

"I think such an outcome of a really scientific world war is by no means improbable. Imagine each side in a position to destroy the chief cities and centers of industry of the enemy; imagine an almost complete obliteration of laboratories and libraries, accompanied by a heavy casualty rate among men of science; imagine famine due to radioactive spray, and pestilence caused by bacteriological warfare: Would social cohesion survive such strains? Would not prophets tell the maddened populations that their ills were wholly due to science, and that the extermination of all educated men would bring the millennium? Extreme hopes are born of extreme misery, and in such a world hopes could only be irrational. I think the great states to which we are accustomed would break up, and the sparse survivors would revert to a primitive village economy.

- "The third possibility, that of the establishment of a single government for the whole world, might be

realized in various ways: by the victory of the
United States in the next world war, or by the
victory of the USSR, or, theoretically, by agreement.
Or—and I think this is the most hopeful of the
issues that are in any degree probable—by an
alliance of the nations that desire an international
government, becoming, in the end, so strong that
Russia would no longer dare to stand out. This
might conceivably be achieved without another
world war, but it would require courageous and
imaginative statesmanship in a number of
countries."

Edith Keeler's imagined future came to pass, of course, in Roddenberry's universe. Humankind did harness incredible energies, and turned toward the stars, and found the unity and resolve to apply its new-found wealth and knowledge and resources to the eradication of those social scourges that plagued our past.

Can we do the same in our own?

Bertrand Russell felt we really have no choice:

"If we are to live together and not die together, we must learn a kind of charity and a kind of tolerance which is absolutely vital to the continuation of human life on the planet."

Sounds like Roddenberry, doesn't he?

"Be as courageous as you can. If none of us is prepared to die for freedom, then all of us will die under tyranny."

~Timothy Snyder

If you enjoyed
Resistance is NOT Futile!,
leave a review on Amazon.com!

See more of
the *Boldly Go!* series
on the following pages!

EXPLORING THE ETHICS OF THE FINAL FRONTIER
STAR TREK
AND HUMANISM
Living by the Star Trek Ethos in a Troubled World
SCOTT ROBINSON
BOLDLY GOING — BOOK #1
What would it take to actually build
the world Star Trek imagined?

Achieving *STAR TREK's* Vision
of the Human Future

CHASING THE
ENTERPRISE

Scott Robinson

In the face of rising authoritarianism, racial tension, greed, and
unchecked nationalism, is there any hope that humanity
can achieve the vision that Star Trek offered?

BOLDLY GOING — BOOK #2

CELEBRATING THE HUMANITY OF THE FINAL FRONTIER

TO SUMMON THE FUTURE

CELEBRATING TREK AND HUMAN SOCIAL PROGRESS

SCOTT ROBINSON

BOLDLY GOING — BOOK #3

12 TREK RULES FOR LIVING
Living the Star Trek Ethos
SCOTT ROBINSON
BOLDLY GOING — BOOK #5

BE LIKE
SPOCK!
ON RELEASING
YOUR INNER VULCAN
SCOTT ROBINSON

The AIs and Androids of
STAR TREK
THE TECHNOLOGY OF THE 23rd CENTURY
AND BEYOND THAT COULD APPEAR IN THE 21st
Scott Robinson

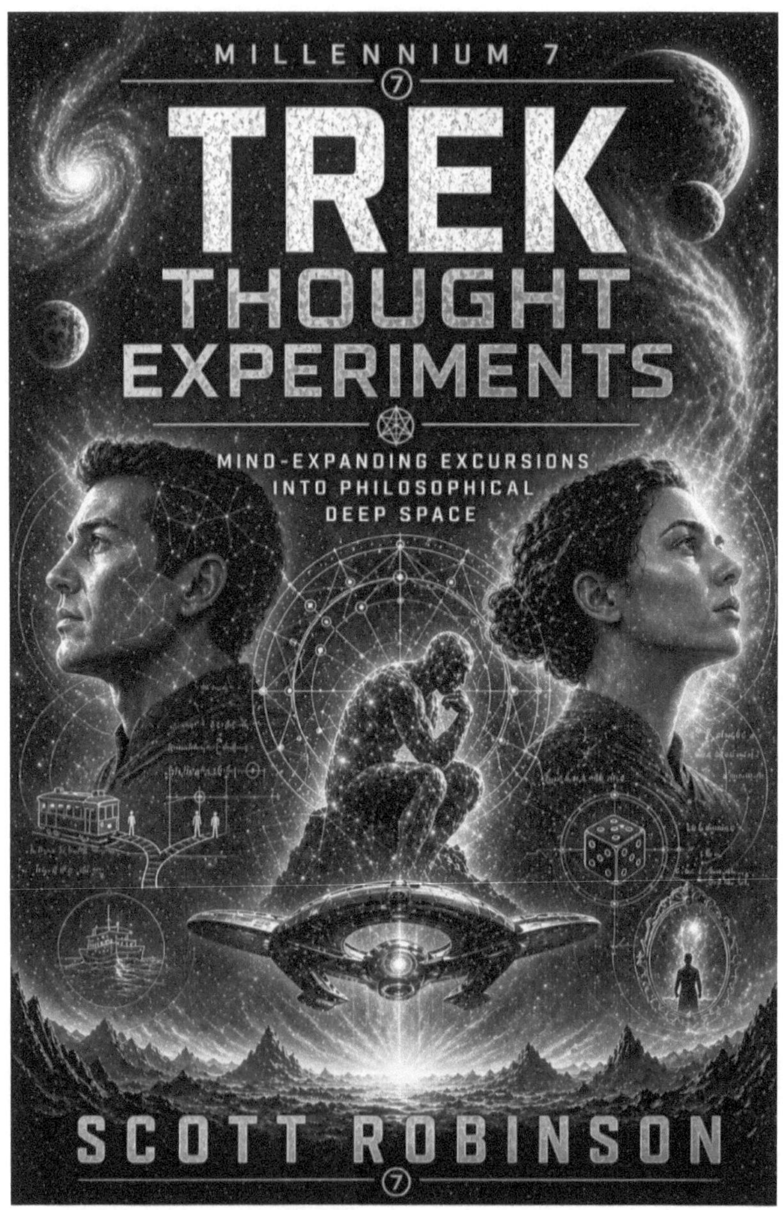
MILLENNIUM 7
7
TREK
THOUGHT
EXPERIMENTS
MIND-EXPANDING EXCURSIONS
INTO PHILOSOPHICAL
DEEP SPACE
SCOTT ROBINSON
7

HAL 9000
HAL 9000
HTT: 6V-12
COM
DV: 30-90
AN
UNAUTHORIZED
BIOGRAPHY
SCOTT
ROBINSON
MANUAL CONTROL
VOICE INPUT
COM
PROG
STOP
EXEC
COMP FUNCT
HIS STATUS
UF STATUS
SYS STATUS
CLEAR

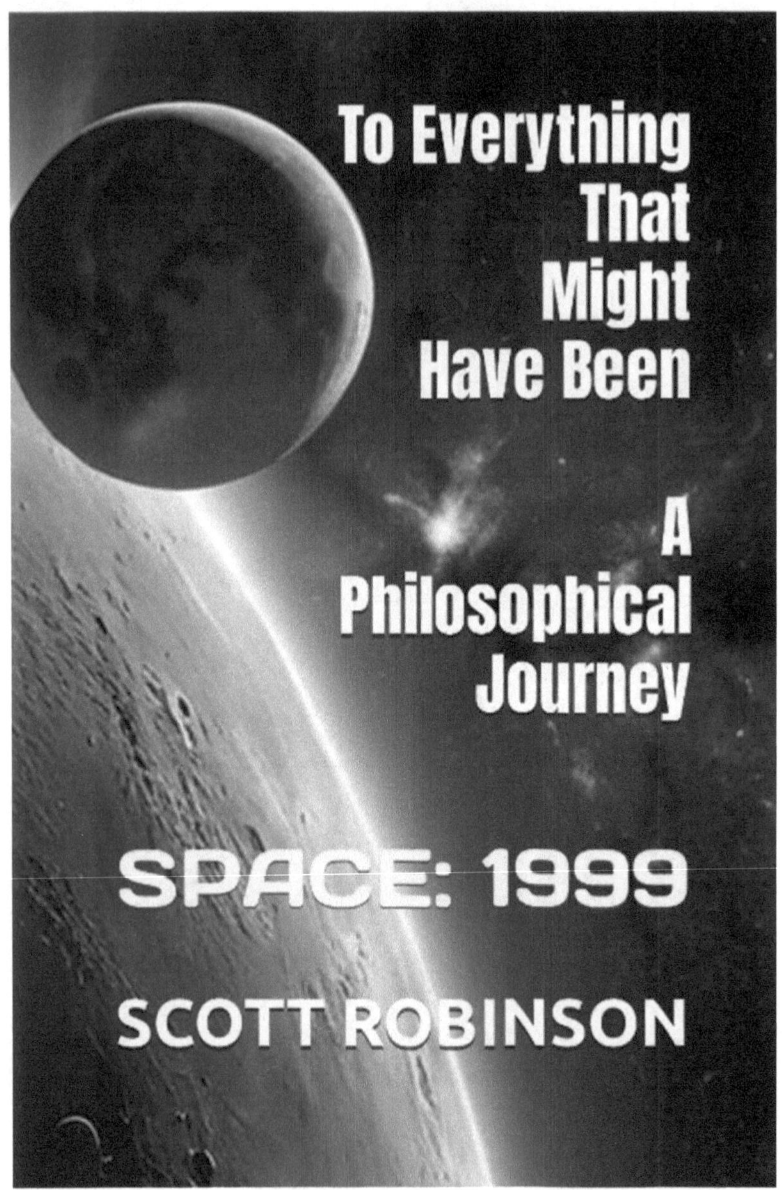
To Everything
That
Might
Have Been

A
Philosophical
Journey

SPACE: 1999

SCOTT ROBINSON

PLURIBUS
JOY & DREAD
IN THE BENEVOLENT MACHINE
SCOTT ROBINSON

Bibliography/Recommended Reading

The Authoritarian Specter, Altemeyer, R. Harvard University Press, 1996.

The Authoritarians, Altemeyer, R. Cherry Hill Publishing, 2009.

The Bill of Obligations: The Ten Habits of Good Citizens, Haass, R. Penguin Press, 2023.

Bowling Alone: The Collapse and Revival of American Community, Putman, R. Simon & Schuster, 2001.

Don't Think of an Elephant! Know Your Values and Frame the Debate, Lakoff, G. Chelsea Green Publishing, 2014.

The Hidden History of American Democracy: Rediscovering Humanity's Ancient Way of Living, Hartmann, T. Berrett-Koehler Publishers, 2023.

The Hidden History of American Oligarchy: Reclaiming our Democracy from the Ruling Class, Hartmann, T. Berrett-Koehler Publishers, 2021.

Metaphors We Live By, Lakoff, G. & Johnson, M. University of Chicago Press, 1994.

On Tyranny: Twenty Lessons from the Twentieth Century, Snyder, T. Tim Duggan Books, 2017.

Red Brains, Blue Brains: Authoritarian We Will Go!, Robinson, S. Paleos Media, 2024.

Red Brains, Blue Brains: The Psychology of MAGA, Robinson, S. Paleos Media, 2024.

Star Trek and Humanism, Robinson, S. Paleos Media, 2023.

To Summon the Future, Robinson, S. Paleos Media, 2023.

ABOUT THE AUTHOR

Scott Robinson is an artificial intelligence designer, social scientist, public speaker and musician, and serves as Director of Technology and Content for the non-profit Humanity Prime. He has been published in *Rolling Stone* and *The Wall Street Journal*. He can be found at

scottrobinsonwriter@gmail.com